How the Bible *Actually* Works*

*In Which I Explain How
an Ancient, Ambiguous,
and Diverse Book Leads
Us to Wisdom Rather
Than Answers—and
Why That's Great News

Peter Enns

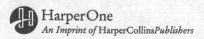

HarperOne
An Imprint of HarperCollinsPublishers

HarperOne

HOW THE BIBLE *ACTUALLY* WORKS. Copyright © 2019 by Peter Enns. All rights reserved. Printed in the United States of America. No part of this book may be used or reproduced in any manner whatsoever without written permission except in the case of brief quotations embodied in critical articles and reviews. For information, address HarperCollins Publishers, 195 Broadway, New York, NY 10007.

HarperCollins books may be purchased for educational, business, or sales promotional use. For information, please email the Special Markets Department at SPsales@harpercollins.com.

FIRST HARPERCOLLINS PAPERBACK EDITION PUBLISHED IN 2020

Illustrations by Shay Bocks. Used with permission.

Library of Congress Cataloging-in-Publication Data is available upon request.

ISBN 978-0-06-268675-6

24 25 26 27 28 LBC 11 10 9 8 7

For Lilah Grace
(aka Lilah Lu, LuLu, Lus, Lilahrama,
The Lu Meister, Baby Girl, Teeny Tiny)
b. 9-30-17
When you are grown up I hope you read all my books.
And Grandpa loves you very much.

Contents

Contents

Contents

Contents

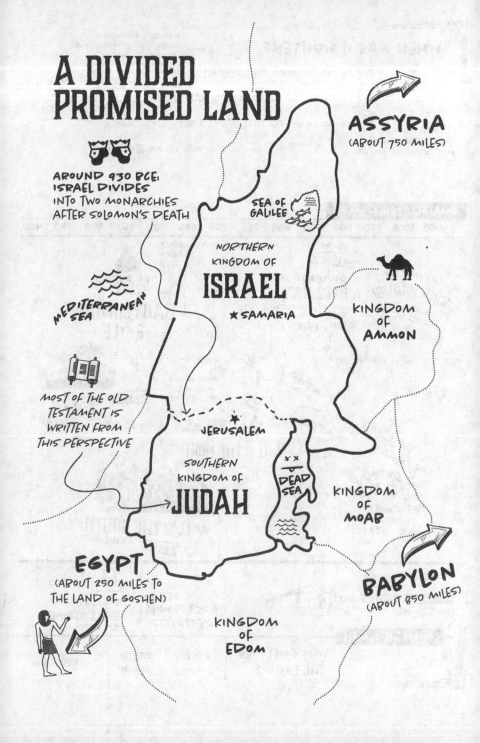

WHEN WAS IT WRITTEN?

CONCERNED WITH ASSYRIAN THREAT AFTER DEPORTATION OF NORTHERN KINGDOM

AROUND 650-600 BCE **DEUTERONOMY** ☒☒☒

NOT LONG AFTER 612 BCE **NAHUM** ▮

2 VERSIONS OF WHAT GOD THINKS ABOUT THE NINEVITES

EARLIEST WRITINGS OF THE OLD TESTAMENT WERE WRITTEN AROUND 1200 BCE

AROUND 630-530 BCE **1 SAMUEL – 2 KINGS** ▭▭▭▭▭▭

SOMETIME AFTER 538 BCE **JONAH** ▮

WHAT HAPPENED WAS...

| 1050 | 1000 | 950 | 900 | 850 | 800 | 750 | 700 | 650 | 600 | 550 | 500 | 450 | 400 |

AROUND 930 BCE

NINEVEH FELL TO BABYLONIANS 612 BCE

586–538 BCE

REIGN OF KING SOLOMON
SOMEWHERE AROUND 970-930

DIVISION OF MONARCHY
GOD'S CHOSEN PEOPLE DIVIDE INTO
NORTH | SOUTH

BABYLONIAN —EXILE—

ISRAEL (NORTH)

JUDAH (SOUTH)

REIGN OF KING MANASSEH 697 - 642 BCE

538 BCE

return OF JUDAH
(AND PERSIAN CONQUEST OF BABYLON)

722 BCE

FALL OF THE NORTH (ISRAEL)

TIME OF KING *David*
SOMEWHERE AROUND 1035 - 970 BCE

THE NORTHERN KINGDOM IS DEPORTED TO ASSYRIA AND IS BASICALLY NEVER HEARD FROM AGAIN

FALL OF THE SOUTH (JUDAH)
586 BCE

SOMEWHERE AROUND 960 BCE ▶
SOLOMON'S TEMPLE BUILT
(FIRST TEMPLE)

586 BCE ▶
FIRST TEMPLE DESTROYED

516 BCE ▶
TEMPLE REBUILT
(SECOND TEMPLE)

FOLLOW THE TEMPLE

| WHO CONTROLS THE LAND? | ASSYRIANS | BABYLONIANS | PERSIANS |

PETE'S PRETTY CLOSE TIMELINE OF BIBLICAL HISTORY

WHO TOLD THE 500-YEAR STORY OF ISRAEL'S MONARCHY BETTER?

1 & 2 CHRONICLES AROUND 350-300 BCE

THE LATEST WRITINGS OF THE NEW TESTAMENT WERE WRITTEN AROUND 100 CE OR A BIT LATER

THE ONLY MENTION OF RESURRECTION IN THE O.T.

DANIEL SOMETIME AROUND 169-164 BCE

350	300	250	200	150	100	50	0	50	100

FOR PERSPECTIVE

JEWISH revolt

PAUL'S MINISTRY AROUND 35 - 57 CE

PAUL IS EXECUTED AROUND 64-67 CE

TIME OF KING david c. 1035 - 970 BCE

3,000 YEARS

AGAINST ANTIOCHUS IV EPIPHANES 167 -160 BCE

332 BCE

YANKEES BEAT METS IN WORLD SERIES IN 5 GAMES 2000 CE

GREEK
CONQUEST OF JUDAH FROM PERSIAN RULE

jesus BORN SOMEWHERE BETWEEN 6-4 BCE

3,000 YEARS

ROLLING STONES FINALLY BREAK UP C. 5000 CE

HEBREW SCRIPTURES TRANSLATED INTO GREEK (**SEPTUAGINT**) BETWEEN 300 - 100 BCE

SECOND TEMPLE PERIOD

HEROD 19 BCE ▶ SERIOUSLY RENOVATED THE TEMPLE

70 CE ▶ SECOND TEMPLE DESTROYED

GREEKS	JEWISH RULE (SORT OF)	ROMANS

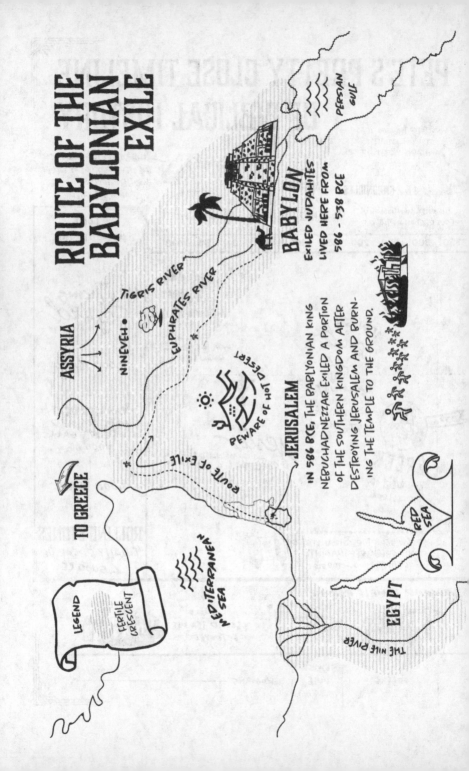

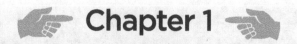

Chapter 1

The Bible's True Purpose

Oh Good. Another Book on the Bible.

To clear the air, let me just put this out there. I am a left-brained academic of German heritage with control issues and marginal social skills. I'm leaving out a few steps, including hours of therapy and self-help seminars, but since I fear you might be losing interest already, let me get to my point.

I've been studying, teaching, and writing about the Bible since the Reagan administration, and—funny thing—I've noticed the same questions keep coming up, not only for me but for plenty others, like:

> What *is* the Bible, exactly?
> Who cares?
> What do I do with it?

and especially:

> How does this ancient, distant, and odd book work for people
> who look to it today for spiritual guidance?

These questions keep coming up because they are not easy to answer. They mean a lot to me, though. They drive what I do.

My last two books lay out common beliefs many Christians have about the Bible that are actually wrong, are not at all biblical, and cause all sorts of spiritual problems. In *The Bible Tells Me So*, I look specifically at the mistaken belief that the Bible is something like a divine instructional manual, a rulebook, so to speak—just follow the instructions as printed and you're good to go. In the follow-up book, *The Sin of Certainty*, I look at a related mistaken notion, namely, the idea that having strong faith is the same thing as feeling certain that the beliefs we hold are correct, and thus periods of doubt or spiritual struggle reveal a weak faith.

When we come to the Bible expecting it to be an instructional manual intended by God to give us unwavering, cement-hard certainty about our faith, we are actually creating problems for ourselves, because—as I've come to see—*the Bible wasn't designed to meet that expectation.* In other words, the "problems" we encounter when reading the Bible are really problems we create for ourselves when we harbor the misguided expectation that the Bible is designed primarily to provide clear answers.

Starting with these mistaken notions causes the whole Christian enterprise to go off course. It causes anxiety and stress about following the Bible's fine print as if it were the "Terms and Conditions" for your latest Apple download, whereas Jesus promises rest to weary pilgrims. And all that stress about needing the Bible to provide certainty about God, life, and the universe is rich soil for cultivating a defensive attitude about our beliefs and therefore an angry and combative posture toward those who see things differently—just another thing to argue about on Facebook, like politics, sports, or who should have won the Oscar.

And maybe that's why a faith that celebrates someone known for his radical agenda of loving one's enemies and turning the other cheek has a public image, according to a number of opinion polls, for being judgmental, condescending, and nasty.

So that's what the other two books are about, and I can't recommend them highly enough. In this book, however, I want to focus not on mistaken beliefs about the Bible and the problems those beliefs cause. Instead, I want to look more closely at the how the Bible actually works. I want to explore how I think God intended the Bible to be used and so to find deeper spiritual benefit in its pages.

Of course, I don't for one minute claim to know what God actually "intends" about anything. I'm not a televangelist or cult leader, claiming special access to the Creator that the rest need to pay for. All I'm going on is what I see the Bible doing, how it behaves when I pay attention to the words in front of me. And when I do that, I see some pretty conspicuous characteristics—three, to be exact—that are not tucked away in a few corners of the Bible, but that are baked into its pages, though they don't always get the airtime they deserve, since they wreak havoc with the aforementioned view that the Bible is a source book for certainty in matters of faith.

Three Surprising Things That Make the Bible Worth Reading

This might be a good time to tell you what these three conspicuous yet often suppressed characteristics of the Bible are: the Bible is *ancient*, *ambiguous*, and *diverse*.

That might sound a bit obscure. I don't blame anyone for expecting me to have used words like *holy*, *perfect*, and *clear*—terms more worthy of the Bible. And those words are fine, I suppose, but not if they paper over how the Bible actually works.

The spiritual disconnection many feel today stems precisely from expecting (or being told to expect) the Bible to be holy, perfect, and clear, when in fact after reading it they find it to be morally suspect, out of touch, confusing, and just plain weird. And they are further told that anything they come across while reading the Bible that threatens this lofty view is either actually no big deal or unfortunate evidence of their own poor reading skills, and neither should get in the way of said lofty view. (Denying the obvious is a great way to create a stressful life for yourself.)

But these three characteristics—*ancient, ambiguous,* and *diverse*— are not rough patches along the way that we need to "deal with," so we can get on with the important matter of reading the Bible properly. They are, rather, what make the Bible *worth reading at all.*

They are not hiding but on full display. They are not obstacles to faith, but characteristics that, if we allow them to chart our course, will let us come to know the Bible in new and spiritually refreshing ways. By embracing these characteristics, we will find a Bible that:

> Challenges and cheers us on as we walk our own difficult path of faith;
>
> Doesn't close windows and lock doors to keep us in, but invites us to risk, to venture forth beyond what is familiar to us, and to seek God directly;
>
> Gently urges us to see through and past the words on the page to what God is up to right here and now;
>
> Encourages and helps us to step out and find God for ourselves.

So what of these three conspicuous yet often suppressed characteristics of the Bible? To say the Bible is *ancient* might seem mundane and unnecessary to point out, but I find the opposite is true. The Bible, because it is a constant companion of faith, is often thought of as "God's personal love letter to me" or the like. But that familiarity risks obscuring how old the Bible really is.

We are as distant from the time of King David (three thousand years ago, about 1000 BCE) as we are from the far distant future time of 5000 CE. Go back another thousand years earlier if you want to start at the time of Israel's most ancient ancestors, Abraham and Sarah. On one level, when we read the Bible, we need to bridge that distance, which is fine, but we still need to respect that distance. Otherwise the Bible can become *too* familiar, too much like us—too comfortable.

We can open the Bible almost at random and begin reading, and it won't take long before we see how deeply embedded the Bible is in this distant and utterly foreign world. In fact, any decent study Bible (a Bible that comes with explanatory footnotes) will point that out by the time we get through the first two sentences of the Bible (Gen. 1:1–2). The ancient writer describes the "beginning" not as a "nothing" or a "singularity," as cosmologists call the pre–big bang state, but as a dark primordial chaos, called *the deep*, which is something like a threatening vast cosmic ocean that God has to tame.

And that sounds weird—which is my point.

If we're paying attention, turning a blind eye to the Bible's ancientness cannot be sustained for long; the distance between now and then needs to be respected as a key character trait of the Bible we have. The writers of the Bible lived long ago and far away, intent on asking *their* questions and seeking *their* answers, oblivious to our own questions and concerns. Now this may seem as if the Bible is locked forever in its ancient moment, but that is most definitely not true.

As we will see, the Bible's antiquity shows us the *need to ponder God anew in our here and now.* Indeed, it gives us permission to do so.

And that's nothing new. As we will see later in the book, Jews and Christians throughout history have always known that this ancient Bible cannot simply be "followed" like a recipe. It takes creative imagination to bridge the ancient and modern horizons. And, as we will see in due course, that process is already happening—I can't stress this enough—*within the pages of the Bible itself.* So instead of trying to pretend this time gap between our day and biblical times doesn't exist, we should embrace this characteristic and let it chart our path.

By *ambiguous* I mean that the Bible, perhaps surprisingly, doesn't actually lay out for anyone what to do or think—or it does so far less often than we have been led to believe. When it comes to the details of what it means to live a life of faith, the Bible doesn't hand out answers just because we are pounding at the door.

Rather, when reading the Bible for spiritual guidance, we find we are usually left to work things out for ourselves at the end of the day. This isn't a drawback or a problem. This is by design. And the thing is, the need to work things out has always been the case, ever since there has been a Bible. So instead of being fed up and frustrated with a Bible that refuses to tell us clearly what to do, maybe we should step back and ask why this is so and what benefit we might derive from it.

And the Bible is *diverse*—meaning it does not speak with one voice on most subjects, but conflicting and contradictory voices. It may feel shocking or disloyal to speak of the Bible this way, but the diversity is actually hard to miss, especially if we read large sections of the Bible in one sitting.

This diversity exists for one simple reason: the Bible was written by various writers who lived at different times, in different places, and under different circumstances and who wrote for different purposes. Their writings demonstrate to us with blinding clarity that they were human beings like us whose perceptions of God and their world were shaped by who they were and when they lived. People of faith have walked this same spiritual path ever since.

So instead of going though painful intellectual contortions pretending this diversity does not exist in the Bible, we should ask why there is so much of it and how this might actually be good news for us.

I don't mean to start off by giving the wrong impression. It might appear that by speaking of an ancient, ambiguous, and diverse Bible I am aiming to focus on what's wrong with the Bible, to point out problems that ought to be overcome, avoided, or at least minimized. But I hope it's clear that my intention is the exact opposite.

I believe that God knows best what sort of sacred writing we need. And these three characteristic ways the Bible behaves, rather than posing problems to be overcome, are telling us something about how the Bible actually works and therefore what the Bible's true purpose is—and the need to align our expectations with it.

God's Plan A: Wisdom

What, then, is the Bible's true purpose when we take seriously its antiquity, ambiguity, and diversity? And with that question we are getting to the main point of this book.

Rather than providing us with information to be downloaded, the Bible holds out for us *an invitation to join an ancient, well-traveled, and sacred quest to know God, the world we live in, and our place in it.* Not abstractly, but intimately and experientially.

A quest—meaning this is going to take some time and effort. No "Have a Great Spiritual Life in Five Easy Steps!" pamphlet. The Bible isn't just going to hand us the goods.

I'm not suggesting that the Bible doesn't provide us with *any* information to enlighten and inspire us or *any* answers to help mark our path. It does, and I trust that will become clear enough as we move along. I only mean that it also provides us with another kind of information that (appreciate the irony) shows us that "providing information" and "giving answers" is not the Bible's true purpose.

After all, if the Bible's true purpose were to provide us with rule-book information about what God is like and what God wants from us, then why can the Bible be so easily used to:

Justify both slavery *and* its abolition?

Justify both keeping women subordinate to men *and* fully emancipating them?

Justify violence against one's enemies *and* condemn it?

Justify political power *and* denounce it?

Both sides of these (and many other) issues have been embraced with uncompromising passion throughout the course of history by real people, convinced they were simply following the Bible's "clear teaching." But if polar opposite positions can keep claiming the Bible's support, then perhaps providing "clear teaching" might not be what scripture is prepared to do. Just throwing that out there.

The Bible, it seems to me, was never intended to work as a step-by-step instructional manual. Rather, it presents us with an invitation to explore. Or better, the Bible, simply by being its ancient, ambiguous, and diverse self, blocks us from the simple path of seeking from it clear answers and rather herds us toward a more subtle, interesting, and above all sacred quest.

That quest is summed up in one beautiful, deep, too often neglected, but absolutely central and liberating biblical idea that shapes everything I have to say in this book: *wisdom*.

Wisdom isn't some secret key available only to an elite few, but the exact opposite. Wisdom is a gift from God, liberally available to all. It is, as we'll see, a "part" of God that saturates every square inch of the world around us and at the same time invades even the hidden places of our heart, those things we like to keep from others, in order to mold and form us into mature children of God.

To put it in Christian terms, wisdom is what forms us to be more like Jesus, who, as the apostle Paul put it, *became for us wisdom from God* (1 Cor. 1:30).

Shepherding us toward wisdom, kicking and screaming if need be: that is the Bible's purpose.

The Bible becomes a confusing mess when we expect it to fulfill some other purpose—like functioning as an owner's manual for faith. But when we allow the Bible to determine our expectations, we see that intending to gain wisdom is our proper spiritual posture toward it.

Wisdom isn't about flipping to a topical index so we can see what we are to do or think—as if the Bible were a teacher's edition textbook with the answers supplied in the back. Wisdom is about the lifelong process of being formed into mature disciples, who wander well along the unscripted pilgrimage of faith, in tune to the all-surrounding thick presence of the Spirit of God in us and in the creation around us.

Rulebook answers deliver certitude and finality, but wisdom embraces mystery.

Rulebook answers are distant and passive, but wisdom is intimate and learned through experience.

Rulebook answers are immediate, but wisdom takes trial and error over time.

Rulebook answers provide comfort and stability, but wisdom asks us to risk letting go of what is familiar for God's surprises.

Rulebook answers are designed to end the journey, but wisdom shapes us so we journey with courage and peace.

Rulebook answers are limited to specific moments, but wisdom works in all times and places.

Rulebook answers keep us small, but wisdom gives us the space we need to grow.

Embracing rather than avoiding the Bible's antiquity, ambiguity, and diversity is like shining a light in a dark room, showing us that the Bible is a book of wisdom rather than prescribed answers, and inviting us to accept the sacred responsibility of pursuing wisdom and thereby learning to live well in God's creation.

Wisdom is not the easy way, but neither is it a burden. Wisdom is freedom, freedom to pursue the Creator, who—as the book of Proverbs puts it—created all things by wisdom.

Wisdom shows us something of the nature of God, so much so

that, for some ancient Jews, to speak of one is to speak of the other. And early Christians fused wisdom together with Jesus—to look on one is to look on the other.

And this wisdom is held out before us in the Bible as a gift of God, not a consolation prize, a Plan B we begrudgingly settle for when the Bible falls short of passing out an answer key, so we know beforehand which ovals to fill in on the standardized test.

A life of pursuing wisdom *is* Plan A.

God Is Not a Helicopter Parent

Even though I promised not to focus on wrong ways of thinking about the Bible, I do need to bring one up here because it is so common, typically hidden just beneath the surface, and it undermines the Bible's work as a book of wisdom.

On orientation day, when my youngest of three children started junior high school, the principal told a captive audience of nervous, success-oriented parents that we help our children best when we resist the urge to become *helicopter parents*, parents who "hover over" and direct every aspect of their kids' lives so they can "succeed." Wise parents know that their job is to equip their children to be independent, to acquire skill sets for navigating on their own the ups and downs of life, to experience failure and triumph, pain and joy, and everything in between, and handle it all well—in other words, to be in training to become mature, well-functioning adults.

Helicopter parents really care more about themselves than their children. They are also objectively the most annoying life-forms on the planet—"helping" their kids with their homework and science-fair projects, running interference with coaches and teachers so Cody and Ashton can make varsity and get into Harvard or Yale. I'm happy to say I did a great job avoiding at least this parenting disaster, mainly because my kids threatened to put me in an "elder care facility" in the North Pyongan Province if I tried anything funny. But I digress.

Although we might not see it, many of us have been taught, in one way or another, that the Bible is our instructional manual and that God is helicoptering over us to make sure we stick to it. And we have been told that if we read this instructional manual carefully, it will inform us on any topic we need an answer to: climate change, parenting, finances, human sexuality, gun control, evolution, which candidate to vote for, whom to marry, whether to buy or rent, where to go to college, what career path to take, what church to go to, what books to read, whether to be vegan, whether to recycle, and so on.

We have practically been conditioned to expect God to be our helicopter parent. And if for some reason we don't run to God to solve every little problem, from finding our car keys to deciding on color schemes for the nursery, we are told there is something deeply wrong with us spiritually. Phooey.

Judging by the fact that our ancient, ambiguous, and diverse Bible is nothing at all like a Christian owner's manual and that, likewise, the life of faith, from the minute we get out of bed in the morning until we hit the pillow at night, is rarely clear and straightforward, I have come to the conclusion that (drumroll) God is not a helicopter parent—which is good because, as I said, helicopter parents are objectively annoying.

If God were a helicopter parent, our sacred book would be full of clear, consistent, unambiguous information to take in. In other words, it wouldn't look anything like it does. But if the Bible's main purpose is to form us, to grow us to maturity, to teach us the sacred responsibility of communing with the Spirit by walking the path of wisdom, it would leave plenty of room for pondering, debating, thinking, and the freedom to fail. And that is what it does.

Judging by how the Bible behaves, God is not a stressed-out helicopter parent, living through his or her children, nervously and fretfully hovering over us in the form of the Bible to make sure we stick to the script, so it all works out. God is a wise parent, prodding us toward spiritual maturity in a secure atmosphere of unconditional love and acceptance, so we can learn to navigate life well. That's what good parents do.

The Bible holds out for us an invitation to accept this timeless and sacred responsibility of working out for ourselves what faith in God looks like here and now, of owning the process, with no accompanying checklist of one-size-fits-all solutions, no safety net of prescripted responses, and no fear that God will bring down the hammer on us for accepting the challenge of faith.

You Are Not Alone

I can say, with the benefit of 20/15 hindsight over thirty years, that nothing has given fresh life to my faith more than letting go of the familiar expectation of security or certainty from the Bible (which is always momentary and eventually falls apart) and—ironically—simply paying careful attention to the Bible and accepting what I see there.

When we are too committed to harboring and sheltering our

familiar false expectations, the Bible itself has a wonderful knack of disrupting those expectations, challenging our categories, and, if need be, agitating our complacency. And the Bible does this simply by—I will say it again—being its ancient, ambiguous, and diverse self, oblivious to our expectations, so ill-suited as a field guide for faith, so reluctant to be co-opted by our questions and the agendas that drive them.

This book is about carving out a truly biblical path, so we can take our faith seriously enough to own it, rather than succumbing to the elaborate and nervous structures of faith that others determine for us. The fact that we have a Bible does not free us from this sacred responsibility, but, as we shall see, demands that we accept that responsibility—and do so as an expression of faith, not a rejection of it.

As I said, I have skin in the game. I have often wondered what shape my Christian life would have taken had I been encouraged from early on, especially during my high-school years, to look to the Bible not primarily as a source of timeless information ready to be downloaded without reservation or question, but as an invitation to a lifelong journey soaked in divine wisdom.

What attitude toward the Bible do we bring to this life of Christian faith, and how do we see God in the process? That's what this book is really about.

Seeing the Bible as a source of godly wisdom to be explored, pondered, deliberated, and put into action will free us of a common burden so many Christians have unwittingly carried, namely, that watching over us is God, an unstable parent, who is right off the bat harsh, vindictive, at best begrudgingly merciful, and mainly interested in whether we've read and understood the fine print; if not, God has no recourse but to punish us.

Seeing the Bible as a wisdom book allows us to see God as a good parent, full of grace, love, and patience—the very character traits we value in earthly parents and that the people of God are to exemplify. Wisdom heals us to see God as God is.

Wisdom also frees us to hold our thoughts about God, life, and the universe with an open hand rather than clenched fist, to face our questions and fears with the focus of a seasoned explorer facing the unknown. We are human, after all, and will always have thoughts about God and the life of faith. And when the Bible is seen as a source of wisdom rather than an instruction manual of universally clear and consistent "teachings," we will learn to be comfortable with the provisional nature of how we think about God and therefore not shy away from interrogating our own faith with gentle candor.

Indeed, we will see that very process as a prompting of God, not an attempt to get out of doing what the Bible says. Adopting a wisdom mentality rather than a rulebook mentality gives us a Bible with fresh possibilities. It leads us to different ways of reading it and appropriating its message.

I know I'm not the only one out there who has felt the need to find better ways of reading the Bible. I wrote this book because no one seems to be explaining the Bible in ways that would have helped me, my family, my friends, my students, and many others I have known over the last few decades.

This book, therefore, is not for the hierarchy who guard the status quo at all costs and brand explorers as unfaithful.

This book is for the *frustratedly* Christian—who have seen that the Bible doesn't meet the expectations they have been taught to cling to and who are having trouble seeing a better way forward.

This book is for the *barely* Christian—who are hanging on to some semblance of faith because they are worn out from having to defend a rulebook Bible.

This book may even be for the *formerly* Christian—who have had the courage to leave their faith behind when it ceased having any explanatory power for their reality because of what they were taught the Bible had to be.

Let me be clear that I don't claim to have crossed over to the promised land, safe from being set upon by pressing questions. If I did claim such a thing, I would simply be peddling one form of certainty over another. The path of wisdom isn't a bigger and better "answer," another version of the same quest for certainty. It's a shift in attitude, a new posture for a lifelong journey of letting go of the need for such things.

Plus, if I claimed to have arrived, I would be lying. As a left-brained, analytical German male, an Enneagram Type Six with control issues,* and (Lord, have mercy) a PhD in biblical studies no less (what was I thinking?), I have no problem saying to anyone who will listen that I live daily with the very difficult tensions of being an unavoidably modern-day human while embracing an ancient faith, rooted in an ancient, ambiguous, and diverse book—which is to say, I continue to have to walk this path of wisdom. I'm not at the beach planted in an Adirondack chair cradling a Corona waiting for the rest of you to show up.

---

* According to the Enneagram Institute (https://www.enneagraminstitute.com/type-6/), we sixes crave structure to alleviate fear. We also tend to be sarcastic. Some famous sixes include Richard Nixon, Mike Tyson, Alex Jones, Rush Limbaugh, and Frodo Baggins. So I have that going for me.

But this book does point in a direction that is spiritually refreshing if also challenging. Better, it is spiritually refreshing because it is challenging. When we choose to walk the path of wisdom, those two will always be joined hand in hand. And that is also the Bible's power—not to bend to our expectations, but to help set them. That's also why, like so many who have taught me, I still find the Bible captivating. I keep seeing new angles to familiar things, or I am shown things I had never noticed before, but, as it turns out, many wise people have.

This Bible just doesn't get old—if we are tuned in to the melody of wisdom.

* * *

In what follows, we will look at how the Bible's antiquity, ambiguity, and diversity, rather than taking something away from the Bible, actually demonstrate to us its true purpose as a book of wisdom rather than a book of rules engraved in stone—and what difference that makes for us. To be sure, we can't cover everything, nor do we need to. By focusing on some portions of the Bible—the wisdom literature, laws, stories, letters, and more—we will see that the Bible's invitation to wisdom is gently persistent and mercifully hounding.

And here's another important dimension of this book. When we accept that biblical invitation, we will see not only how the Bible challenges *us* to work out what it means to live the life of faith here and now. We will also see—if I may stress the point once again—*how the biblical writers themselves were already challenged by the need to move past a rulebook mentality and respond to new circumstances with wisdom.*

Let me say that again. What I'm saying *we* need to do—walk the path of wisdom—the biblical writers were already doing. Biblical writers already accepted the sacred challenge of pursuing a life of wisdom rather than thinking of God as a helicopter parent. We'll revisit this theme throughout the book.

The Bible is designed for wisdom because it reflects the wisdom of God—not despite its antiquity, ambiguity, and diversity, but precisely by means of them. Its purpose is to invite us to explore, ponder, reflect, muse, discuss, debate, and in doing so work out a life of faith—not to keep that hard work from happening.

The Bible is not the problem. The Bible is great—not because it is an answer book, but precisely because it isn't; not because it protectively hovers over us, but because it most definitely doesn't.

The Bible will make that clear to us if we let it.

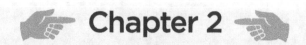

Chapter 2

The Bible Doesn't Really Tell Us What to Do —and That's a Good Thing

Screwing Up Your Kids Biblically

I have a morning routine, and if I don't stick to it, the world will end.

I get up, go downstairs to the kitchen, start the coffee, deal with our rescue cat, Marmalade, who insists on some immediate "me time" while the coffee brews, take my vitamins, and sit at my desk drinking my coffee while repeatedly shoving Marmalade off the keyboard, so I can get some work done. My goal then is to tick off as many boxes on my to-do list as quickly as I can to bring peace and harmony to the universe and so I can feel good about myself.

I confess, most mornings (and the hours that follow) really are about me and reducing stress through task completion. But every now and then the spiritual part of me pushes to the surface, and I wonder what God thinks about how I greet the miracle of yet another new dawn—and I start feeling a bit guilty about being so spiritually dim-witted.

What should I be doing in those little moments that I have chosen to take up with coffee and pushing a cat off my keyboard? What is God thinking about me and my German to-do list mentality right this second? Am I "good enough"? Am I getting it "right"? Is my life lined up with "God's will for my life"? What does that even mean, and how would I know? It's stressful just thinking about it.

Maybe I'm just a fraud, playing a religion game, stuck in this self-centered mess I've made of my life, without a clue that I am plummeting toward destruction.

So that's my morning. How's yours?

And don't even get me started on wondering about how I'm doing in God's eyes with the really *big* things in life that actually matter, like having raised three children and the thousands of no-win, directionless, Hail Mary decisions I made in the process. Maybe you know the drill. Are they overscheduled? Underscheduled? Piano or cello? What type of school is best? What can they watch or listen to and at what age? Should they be let out of the house wearing *that*? When is the right time for a cell phone? With unlimited data? And if that's not enough stress, there's always the college search (and debt) to look forward to. No pressure there.

Speaking for myself, raising children seems to have been set up as a cosmic conspiracy aimed specifically at me to generate stress, second-guessing, and the ever-present sense of panic that I am absolutely screwing my kids up forever because I missed some clear bit of God's plan for this all-important and sacred task of child rearing that everyone else seems to understand but I am too spiritually dull to see.

I sure could have used a divine instruction manual of some sort.

"But we *do* have God's instruction manual for raising children!" some have told me. "It's called the Bible, dummy."

Yes, I have to agree, the Bible does comment now and then on the topic, and I want to take seriously what the Bible has to say.

But here's the problem. The Bible doesn't really help. It's confusing. Parts are actually troubling. Some of it is illegal.

Here is something from the book of Proverbs: *Discipline your children while there is hope* (19:18). That sounds like fear-based parenting. "Hurry up and discipline your kids—early and often—so they don't grow up to be _____ [fill in the blank with your worst nightmare—mine include such things as "professional academic," "internet start-up," and any other line of work in which you need a Kickstarter campaign to feed your family]. How your kids turn out is a reflection on *you* . . . on YOOOU!"

Thank you, Bible! Please, tell me more about child rearing. I can't wait to keep reading more encouraging gems like this.*

Anyway, how would I know when I've reached the point where hope is lost? It would also help tremendously if I knew what "discipline" actually looked like. A time out? Make them memorize Bible verses? Ground them? Send them to boarding school? Labor camp? Make them give both cats a bath at the same time?

Here's another passage from the book of Proverbs, a go-to, slam-dunk favorite of Christian child-rearing experts everywhere: *Train children in the right way, and when old, they will not stray* (22:6).

Again, more fear that parents might not do enough "training." And what does that "training" look like, exactly, and what is "the right way"? Like, that's my whole question. Should they sit up straight? Wash their hands before dinner? Not listen to rock music? Not have sex before marriage? Play travel soccer? And what does it mean, practically speaking, to "stray"? Where is the line between healthy youthful boundary exploration and actual straying?

What do I do?! That's all I want to know.

Reading the book of Proverbs on child rearing is like paying good money for financial advice and being told after ten sessions, "Here's

---

* Sarcasm.

what I've come up with. Invest your money wisely, and you will be set for retirement." I was hoping for stock tips.

Here's a passage from the New Testament addressed to children: *Children, obey your parents in everything, for this is your acceptable duty in the Lord* (Col. 3:20).

"Put your toys away. If you don't, you'll make baby Jesus cry. You don't want to see baby Jesus cry, do you?" Some parents love this one.

Another New Testament letter, the book of Ephesians, adds that honoring your father and mother is the first of the Ten Commandments that comes with a promise: *so that it may be well with you and you may live long on the earth* (6:3). So, the Bible contains death threats?

As a general guideline I believe that children should obey their parents, but as an absolute rule to live by it sounds like a license for child abuse. Are we really meant to conclude that children should *always* obey their parents no matter what—like, every single time, without fail? What if the parents are neo-Nazis—or Calvinists? What if they are drunk or abusive? Should those kinds of parents be obeyed *in everything* as an *acceptable duty in the Lord*?

Is there no room here for pushback or just common sense? Maybe so, but it would certainly help avoid misunderstandings if all these passages began, "Generally speaking . . ." What we read, however, sounds uncomfortably like an unalterable command written by an inspired biblical author taking dictation from God. After all, this is the Bible and when God's word says "obey your parents in everything," who are we to pick and choose?

Or perhaps we readers are meant to insert "generally speaking" and then figure things out on our own as situations come up—in other words, to be wise. That's what I think.

The Bible also includes child-rearing instructions that I have no intention of doing ever. Back to Proverbs: *Do not withhold discipline from your children; if you beat them with a rod, they will not die* (23:13).

I am relieved that beating my child with a rod (aka discipline) will only result in deep bruising and some broken ribs, but not death.* Still, this passage sounds more like a sure ticket to a visit from Child Services than day-to-day godly parenting advice. A disturbing echo can be found in the book of Exodus concerning the treatment of slaves: a slaveholder who strikes a slave with a rod is only punishable if the slave dies right away (21:20). Maybe children, like slaves, are property? That would at least explain this:

> *If someone has a stubborn and rebellious son, . . . his father and his mother . . . shall say to the elders of his town, "This son of ours is stubborn and rebellious. He will not obey us. He is a glutton and a drunkard." Then all the men of the town shall stone him to death.* (Deut. 21:18–21)

Okay, I'm not doing that. Not that I haven't been tempted, but no.

Getting the townsfolk together to stone your son to death for stubbornness seems like the kind of thing civilized societies were created to prevent. And it probably doesn't send a message of unconditional love to the remaining siblings. Probably doesn't make a good evangelistic conversation starter either.

Am I wrong, or is inflicting physical pain as child rearing a recurring theme?

---

* Sarcasm.

I suppose it would have been nice if God had handed us a Bible with a chapter in it called "FAQs on Godly Rules for Parenting" that didn't include capital punishment and told us what the "right way" and "discipline" are, so we didn't crank out little hellions. But that's not what we have.

If the Bible's purpose was to provide for us clear and unchanging direction about basic pressing matters like, "How do I raise my kids well?"—it wouldn't generate so many obvious questions.

I'm not writing a child-rearing book, at least not until my adult children let me know whether they intend to sign the Do Not Resuscitate form, should it ever come to that. I'm just saying that what the Bible says about raising children is ambiguous once we pay attention to the details. It's even morally suspect in places, in *need* of being questioned—even interrogated.

And here is the bigger point of all this: *How the Bible addresses this one topic of child rearing is a window onto how inadequate (and truly unbiblical) a rulebook view of the Bible as a whole is.*

It unravels once you start pulling the thread. The Bible seems intent on pointing us in another direction entirely.

Fools and Finances

Before we move on to the Bible as a whole, let's stay with Proverbs a bit longer—yes, the book we just looked at with all that unhelpful parenting advice. But give it a chance. Proverbs actually makes it loud and clear that seeking wisdom rather than grabbing for answers is what this life of faith is about. Proverbs is a book of wisdom, after all.

Tucked away toward the end of the book of Proverbs, minding their own business, not trying to grab our attention but just waiting to be found, are back-to-back bits of wisdom that completely contradict each other:

> *Do not answer fools according to their folly,*
> *or you will be a fool yourself.*
>
> *Answer fools according to their folly,*
> *or they will be wise in their own eyes.* (26:4–5)

Let me say right here and now that the lesson we learn from these two little verses sums up not only how Proverbs works, but how the Bible *as a whole* works as a book of wisdom. But let's not get ahead of ourselves.

Anyone who hangs out on social media at all knows how effortlessly it can bring out the worst in us. Not me, of course, but everyone else. I'm an angel.

Sometimes the comments are rude, condescending, insulting, passive-aggressive, or baiting. I mean, people *really* get upset over almost everything! And each time that happens, I have to ask myself, "Should I ignore him or let him have it?" (Yes, "him." Ninety-nine percent of the time it's some dude who really needs to find another way to prove his manhood.)

I'd really like some clear divine direction here on how to handle these trolls, but the book of Proverbs, which is supposed to tell us what wisdom looks like, has these two passages side by side that give us two conflicting instructions: "Definitely do *not* answer this fool. Oh, wait. No. Definitely *do* answer him."

Is this multiple choice? Do I just pick one? I just want a snappy phrase that tells me what to do when this happens—like "Stranger, danger," "Stop, drop, and roll," or "In the event of a loss of cabin pressure, place the oxygen mask firmly over your nose and mouth, secure the elastic band behind your head, and breathe normally." Am I asking too much? Apparently.

What makes the ambiguity all the more striking is the topic—fools. This isn't some minor issue, like whether it's finally time to get double-pane windows (you probably should; they will save you hundreds in heating costs and over time will more than pay for themselves). "Fool" in Proverbs is *the* catchall term for someone you definitely do not want to be: a hater of knowledge, a slanderer, one who leads others down the path to destruction, someone who lacks discernment and is complacent, stubborn, ignorant, prideful, greedy, and a whole slew of other despicable character traits.

Today we might call someone like this a total jerk (feel free to supply a more colorful term). Biblically speaking, though, a fool is roughly synonymous with someone who is "ungodly" or "unrighteous"—someone whose actions are out of sync with God's ways and out of harmony with others'. Fools lead you away from God, and so we might expect here of all places, where the topic under consideration is "fools," to get some clear direction about what to do when we come face-to-face with such a disruptive, ungodly person.

But no. Instead we are told (1) not to engage a fool because by doing so you will come down to his level *and* (2) to engage the fool to shut him up.

And so here is my point. These two clearly contradictory proverbs aren't a problem that needs fixing. The biblical writers weren't idiots. Placing these two opposite sayings side by side gives us a snapshot of how wisdom works.

It seems to me that whoever composed this book and placed these proverbs* next to each other was saying at least this: If we are looking to the Bible to be a rulebook, not only will we be frustrated, but we will *miss the wisdom this pairing contains.* Both of these sayings are wise, and the one we act upon here and now, at this unscripted moment, depends on which fits the current situation best.

Reading the *situation*—not simply the Bible—is what wisdom is all about.

It's also, as we'll see, what the life of faith is about.

Sometimes it's best to answer a fool, sometimes not. Which option is best at this unscripted moment depends on all sorts of factors that are impossible to anticipate, and so each time I read a nasty comment, I have to decide in the moment what the best way forward is in *this* situation. Maybe what I am seeing is less anger and more pain and fear, and this person needs a place to vent. Or maybe he's been burned and needs a safe space to let it out. Or maybe the comment just needs to be deleted and the commenter blocked.

The point is that Proverbs 26:4–5 doesn't tell me what to do. It wasn't designed to. It models something better: the permission to

---

* Okay, nerdy footnote coming your way, because I need to drop it in somewhere. You may have noticed my switching back and forth between *proverbs* and *Proverbs.* Uppercase refers to the book of Proverbs. Lowercase refers to one or more of the individual sayings in the book. See, this is why you read the footnotes. To impress your friends. Some of us went to graduate school to learn this.

think it through, figure it out, and learn from experience for next time. In fact, more than just giving us permission, the contradiction sets up our expectation that we will *have* to think it through.

And I'll bet some of you might have thought "contradictions" in the Bible were "bad." They're not. They're revealing.

The Bible doesn't normally lay things out so clearly with side-by-side contradictions. Usually they are spread out over the book. As in the case of wealth.

Wealth—getting it, keeping it, and acquiring more of it—has been an issue for most of recorded civilization, including for the ancient Israelites, judging by how often Proverbs brings it up. Marriages and families are destroyed by it, nations go to war over it, people are exploited so the powerful can hoard it.

I basically suck at wealth. My long-term planning has been a failure. Apparently plugging your ears and singing, "La-la-la-la, I cannot hear you" for three decades and wishing for the best is not a solid financial strategy. And those commercials just make it worse by producing shame—you know, the ones where the annoyingly intimate financial adviser and his client seem to have oodles of time to just hang out over coffee and review his "portfolio"—which, I gather, is how people who have a lot of money refer to "money."

> Thanks for hanging out with me for seven straight hours,
> Tom. I'm just stressed about not being able to turn my
> 1.8 million into 2.2 million by the time I'm thirty-seven.
> After all, as we've discussed, I want to send my kids to
> Harvard, buy a small country, and cheat death. The market
> fluctuation is scary. Hold me.

I understand, Steve, but it'll be okay. Stay latched on to me like a baby monkey. I'll see you through this every step along the way. Text me 24/7. I love you and care for you.

Thank you, Tom. You complete me.

Give me a break.

My one and only recent financial conversation went more like this:

Pete. PETE! Get up. Here's a tissue. Look, it's not all bad news. I project that if you get a second job, keep working until you're ninety-seven, max out every year on every conceivable retirement plan known to humanity, and sell a kidney and one eye on the black market, you'll be able to die in your basement—assuming Social Security, Medicare/Medicaid, and food stamps are still up and running. But just in case, swing by the office and let's talk lottery strategies.

Let's not make this about me (though I think I just did). I'm only saying that, speaking from personal experience, a godly attitude toward wealth seems, again, like an absolutely ideal topic to get some clarity on, and you'd think a book like Proverbs that's supposed to provide wisdom would hit this one out of the park.

But no. Instead, we see that wealth is both a blessing and a curse, a security and a danger. It all depends. Compare two more verses from Proverbs:

> *The wealth of the rich is their fortress;*
> *the poverty of the poor is their ruin.* (10:15)

The wealth of the rich is their strong city;
in their imagination it is like a high wall. (18:11)

Like Proverbs 26:4–5, these two proverbs force us to ponder what a proper attitude toward wealth looks like, especially since, like the "fools" proverbs above, they begin with exactly the same words,* but then go in opposite directions. That tension created by the book of Proverbs is never resolved.

It's not meant to be.

The lesson here is that wealth can be positive or negative, depending on our attitude. A razor-thin line exists between genuine thankfulness to God for the protection wealth can provide and arrogance about one's wealth. The book of Proverbs challenges us to get used to patrolling that line, so we can learn when we cross it.

And neither of these proverbs should be elevated above the other as the Bible's clear and final teaching on wealth. Neither the TV preacher who thinks God told him to definitely get a third Learjet nor extremists who think that having a savings account is sinful is exercising wisdom.

We need to use our heads here, people—which is precisely what these contradictory passages in Proverbs are driving us toward. We are left to read the situation to see which bit of wisdom fits here and now.

Proverbs doesn't do the heavy lifting for us. It alerts us that *we* have to. We cannot escape that sacred responsibility—ever.

---

* Another nerd alert. "Fortress" in 10:15 and "strong city" in 18:11 are the same in Hebrew, *qirith 'uzzo*, literally "strong city (or town)." I'm honestly not sure why this phrase was translated differently in these two verses.

My Big Point, and Then an Even Bigger Point

Proverbs can be deceptive. All those little sayings, neatly lined up one after another. They just *look* like "rules to live by." But knowing what to do is about much more than reading words on the page. It's about learning to read the moment, those day-in-and-day-out gray situations that befall us without forewarning—like how to handle nasty comments or what to spend your money on. Contradictory proverbs about fools and finances neatly capture this truth.

Doing the best as we can to figure out life, to discern how or if a certain proverb applies right here and now, is not an act of disloyalty toward God, rebellion against God's clear rulebook for life. It is, rather, our sacred responsibility as people of faith. Proverbs drives us toward that insight by being steeped in those three characteristics we glimpsed earlier: antiquity, ambiguity, and diversity.

Proverbs is *diverse*, as we just saw concerning fools and finances. It gives not a single point of view, but two extremes—and everything in between—suited for countless situations.

Proverbs is also *ambiguous*, for it is short on details, like how to raise children. We are left to fill in the details. Further, a book of wisdom that advises beating your child with a rod (or stoning to death a rebellious teenager, as we saw in Deuteronomy*) raises another sort

---

* Deuteronomy, though technically not wisdom literature, nevertheless bears the mark of wisdom "influences," as scholars like to put it, such as Moses's admonishment to the people to *give heed* to the teachings he is giving them (Deut. 4:1), which echoes such passages as Proverbs 1:8 and 10:17 about "hearing" or "heeding" wise instruction. Anyway, that's why I feel I have permission to include a passage from Deuteronomy in a chapter that focuses on Proverbs. That, and I just feel like it. Plus it signals that what we are seeing here with regard to Proverbs holds elsewhere.

of ambiguity, namely, whether these sorts of proverbs have any abiding value for us.

No question, Proverbs makes you think. And no matter how carefully we read almost any other proverb, we face similar ambiguities. Seriously. Open up Proverbs, randomly put your finger down on the page, and try to explain to the person next to you what that proverb means. Exactly.

We read in Proverbs 25:11: *A word fitly spoken is like apples of gold in a setting of silver.* It looks like we're talking about some sort of ornate platter (?), but why are golden apples in a setting of silver such a big deal in the first place, and what does that have to do with me right now? Nor is it spelled out what a *word fitly spoken* looks like or what that has to do with a platter.

This example also shows how the ambiguities in Proverbs are often tied to the book's *antiquity*. When we read Proverbs, we are crossing a chasm of time and culture. The methods of disciplining children we've seen most certainly reflect the rather harsh climate of Iron Age tribal culture (1200–500 BCE), where physical violence among peoples and nations is a ho-hum matter-of-fact reality. Even God is depicted as a warrior who ruthlessly slays the enemy.*

We don't live then, but now. How bound are we, then, to the Bible's child-rearing instructions?

More to the point, Proverbs wasn't written for twenty-first-century Western churchgoing suburbanites. Though the deep origins of the book remain a mystery, Proverbs was likely compiled for the purpose of training young upper-class Israelite men for a life of

---

* As in Exodus 15, a song celebrating Israel's deliverance from Egyptian slavery, which begins, *The LORD is a warrior. . . . Pharaoh's chariots and his army he cast into the sea* (read "drowned"; 15:3–4).

royal service. This is why the book is throughout addressed to sons (not daughters) and gives due weight to topics that would be most relevant for a ruling class—like wealth and justice (for example, Prov. 1:3; 2:8).

This book was designed for an ancient ruling class, but here's the twist. Centuries later, this book was eventually included in the Bible of Judaism (the Christian Old Testament).* Long before Christianity came to be, Proverbs was already "democratized," that is, transformed from a book for some to a book for everyone.

In other words, the simple fact that Proverbs later came to be included in the for-everyone book we call the Bible speaks volumes—it means that those ancient Jews who made that decision saw in it *value beyond the reason for which it was originally written.*

So, here's my point. We do not share the ancient setting of the original audience of Proverbs. When we read it, we have to transpose it into another key if we hope to connect with it. In fact, the book's very inclusion in the collection of for-everyone books is already a significant transposition. Otherwise this ancient book would forever remain an artifact from the past, a decaying monument to a long-ago time and a faraway place.

Because Proverbs was included in a collection of sacred books meant for all, it now flies off the pages of its ancient origins and invites us to bring it into our own time and place—ruler, peasant, and everyone in between.

---

* I often use the common Christian term "Old Testament" when referring to the Bible of Judaism. Since the Christian Bible is different than the Jewish Bible (the Christian Bible has all that Jesus stuff in there), using "Old Testament" will help avoid unnecessary confusion about what part of the Christian Bible I am talking about. I mean no disrespect to Judaism or to its scripture, which I trust is already clear.

That is how Proverbs works, and with that, now is as good a time as any to repeat my really big point in all of this about where we are heading: Proverbs models for us *how the Bible as a whole works.*

The entire Bible, like Proverbs, is ancient, ambiguous, and diverse. *The Bible as a whole demands the same wisdom approach as Proverbs.*

Once we come to see the entire Bible as a book of wisdom, we will come to know a Bible that opens up for us a deeper, more life-affirming, and frankly more captivating journey of faith than one that is preoccupied with coloring inside the lines.

When reading the Bible—not just Proverbs—we never escape the responsibility of having to ask ourselves, "How does this connect to here and now, to my specific circumstances?" And, as I said, the answer to that question is never simply a matter of reading the book as if following a list of unalterable instructions, but of reading the moment.

The Bible is a book of wisdom and so funnels us toward taking responsibility to remain open and curious about what it means to live life in the presence of God.

And an Even Bigger (and Final) Point

I still understand that seeing the Bible this way might cause some a bit of concern. I get it. After all, if the Bible is God's word to us but isn't clear and direct, what good is it? If we see the Bible as a book of wisdom that makes us figure things out rather than dispensing unambiguous divine instruction shaped for our eyes and ears, it may seem like we're caving in to a "less than" view of the Bible that isn't of much practical use for anyone—a Plan B because Plan A unraveled.

But again, nothing could be farther from the truth. Wisdom *is* Plan A. Is it ever.

Proverbs goes out of its way to make sure we see that wisdom is worthy of our full attention, deserving of a central place in our approach to faith. Proverbs does this by tying wisdom to creation itself.

For one thing, Proverbs puts wisdom in the Garden of Eden. Wisdom, we are told, is *a tree of life to those who lay hold of her** (3:18).

In the story of Adam and Eve (Gen. 2–3), we read that God forms Adam out of earth, breathes life into him, and then gives him one and only one command: *You may freely eat of every tree of the garden; but of the tree of the knowledge of good and evil you shall not eat, for in the day that you eat of it you shall die* (2:16–17). As the story goes, Eve is soon tricked by a crafty serpent to take a bite of fruit from the tree. She then gives it to Adam—who apparently had been standing there all along watching this transaction happen—and he takes a bite.

And so they die. Only they don't . . . But they do.

What actually happens is that the unlucky couple is *driven out of the garden—exiled,* as it were—so that they might be barred from partaking of the tree of life. Having access to the tree of life is symbolic of spiritually being in God's presence. Death means being alienated from God.

We see life and death used the same way in other passages in the Bible, which likewise speak of being "driven out" of somewhere—namely, the land of Israel. In Ezekiel 37:1–14, Judah's exile to Babylon is a "death," and the nation is depicted as a mass of dry, lifeless human

---

* In Hebrew, the word for "wisdom" (*hokmah*) is grammatically feminine and therefore personified as a woman, hence "her." More on this in a minute.

bones that God brings to "life" (brings back to the land). Likewise, Deuteronomy 30:11–20 promises "life" in the land as a blessing for obedience and "death" outside of the land (exile) for disobedience.

Wisdom as a "tree of life" in Proverbs is the solution to this problem of "death," of alienation from God. Wisdom opens up the gates of Paradise and gives us back access to life that was lost. Not life literally, but symbolically—a quality of life, a life in harmony with God and creation.

Now, I know that alert Christian readers may balk a bit at this. Drawing us to God is supposed to be Jesus's role. He is the Savior. I get it. But the New Testament ties Jesus to wisdom, which we'll definitely get to later. All I am saying here is that wisdom in the Old Testament is a big deal because of what it is able to do—or better, undo: the curse of "exile" on Adam and Eve.

Proverbs also ties wisdom farther back to the dawn of time: *The LORD by wisdom founded the earth; by understanding he* established the heavens* (3:19). What it means for God to have founded the earth *by wisdom* is hardly obvious, but we don't need to try to work it all out. It's enough to observe that wisdom and creation are inseparable—without wisdom, there is no creation.

Proverbs 8:22–31 has more to say about it. Here wisdom is depicted as a female character who declares that she was beside God in the act of creation, rejoicing when God formed the earth, heavens, oceans,

---

* In the Bible, God is typically (though not absolutely always) depicted as male. For the record, I don't think God is gendered, and I try my best to avoid using male pronouns, but when I am citing biblical passages that refer to God as Yahweh (a male deity), or if avoiding the male pronoun would result in some painfully awkward sentence structures, I will say he, him, or his. I think that's the best solution until English comes up with agreed-upon pronouns that transcend gender. But I have a writing deadline.

springs, mountains, and fields. Creation—all there is, which we humans cannot fathom—is God's grand act of wisdom, so to speak.

And that's why wisdom for our daily lives is worth seeking and heeding!

When we seek to live our lives "by wisdom," we are participating in the "life force" by which God created the universe. You may have a less Star Warsy way of putting it, but it's the best I can do on short notice.

When instead of simply reacting to a jerk coworker or an internet troll, we pause and calmly seek wisdom for that moment, even if imperfectly (for surely we are all on the journey of gaining wisdom), we are tapping into something big that created and sustains the cosmos. We are in a sense cocreating with the Creator—not bringing the cosmos into existence (obviously), but creating our own life path by the choices we make.

That's why I think of living a life of wisdom as a "sacred responsibility." It is a *responsibility* because God is not a helicopter parent. And it is *sacred* because all of our efforts, big and small, to live wisely are sacred acts of bowing to and seeking alignment with the Wise Creator.

And so when we do the kinds of things Proverbs goes on and on about, like holding our tongue, refusing to answer back, being patient, speaking tenderly, putting the needs of others before our own, doing a thoughtful and kind deed, we are aligning with the life force that echoes back to the foundation of all there is.

So, again, wisdom is sort of a big deal.

In fact, Proverbs 8:22–31 adds quite a remarkable twist to all this. Wisdom seems not to have been created by God, like everything else, but "acquired" by God and "born" of God *before* the act of creation (see verses 22–24).* Language like this led some ancient Jewish readers (before the time of Jesus) to an interesting possibility. Since wisdom was acquired or born *before* creation, wisdom would be as close to God as you can get. Of course, we have to remember that this is all metaphorical language, a way of talking about wisdom as a basic characteristic of the Creator. But one Jewish text written near the time of Jesus, the Wisdom of Solomon, took this idea to its logical conclusion.**

In chapter 10, this author describes wisdom as doing things that the Old Testament attributes to God—like creating Adam, delivering the Hebrew slaves from Egypt, and a number of other things. That doesn't mean this ancient author actually equated God and wisdom, but, taking his cue from Proverbs 8, God and wisdom are like two peas in a pod. For this author wisdom is God's breath, the ruler of the world, seated by God's throne.

All this is very interesting (to me, at least) but let's get to why I am taking up a couple of paragraphs talking about it. Building off of Proverbs 8, at least some ancient Jews ascribed to wisdom something approaching divine status to act as a mediator between God and humanity, to make God accessible to us here and now.

---

* In verse 22, many English translations have *created* instead of "acquired," though they also supply a footnote explaining that "acquired" is the better translation.

** The Wisdom of Solomon is a moving book written to encourage Jews to remain faithful amid persecution. It wasn't written by Solomon—it was actually written in Greek either slightly before or during the first century CE—and for that reason is not included in Jewish or Protestant Bibles, but consigned to a collection of sixteen books referred to by the tantalizing title Apocrypha, a Greek word meaning "hidden" (though apparently not particularly well). The book is included, however, in the Bibles of the Orthodox and Roman Catholic churches along with other Apocryphal books, a number of which will come up later.

That's the key point for us: *accessible*.

Times had changed for this author. The days of old, when prophets and inspired writers walked among them, was over. But wisdom was still there as she always was, even from the very beginning of creation. And the Wisdom of Solomon goes on to say that wisdom enters human souls and makes them *friends of God, . . . for God loves nothing so much as the person who lives with wisdom* (7:27–28).

This ancient Jewish text is already articulating for us what I've been getting at for some pages now: to know God is to live with wisdom, who is *more beautiful than the sun, and excels every constellation of the stars* (Wisd. of Sol. 7:29).

Wisdom became a prominent image for Judaism, which sets the stage for how the New Testament writers processed the idea of wisdom through a Jesus lens—the place held by wisdom would now be held by Jesus, "God with us," who, as Paul put it, *became for us wisdom from God* (1 Cor. 1:30). And this divine force by which all things were created, called "the Word" in John's Gospel, clearly echoes wisdom's role in Proverbs 8:

> *In the beginning was the Word, and the Word was with God, and the Word was God. He was in the beginning with God. All things came into being through him, and without him not one thing came into being.* (John 1:1–3)

We'll get back to Judaism and Jesus soon enough. I only mention it here briefly to let us glimpse how big a deal wisdom is in Proverbs, in early Judaism, and among the early followers of Jesus. And more important, whether we are talking about wisdom or Jesus, the end benefit is to make humans "friends of God."

Living in harmony with God and others amid the complex and changing circumstances of history and how we live in our time and place simply don't happen according to a script. When we seek to live by wisdom, we will quickly see the need to move beyond the words on the page in order to make them our own. And when we do that, we embrace the mystery of faith by tapping into the life force of creation itself.

So, once again, wisdom is God's Plan A. Anything else, which includes thinking of the life of faith as primarily a script to follow verbatim, is settling for something "less than."

The Little and Hidden Things

No one wakes up in the morning and thinks, "Yes, today I'll work on greed. I will address that problem between the hours of 9:00 a.m. and noon, and then after lunch I'll move on to tackle pride between 1:00 and 3:00." I suppose someone might approach life like this, or at least try, but such a person will soon find out, by about 9:05, that life just happens and you have to be ready to be wise in the moment, whatever is called for: watch what you say to your children; don't let that compliment go to your head; think carefully how you engage a fool; be careful how you view money.

Wisdom is about being trained to be ready for the little and hidden things, the unscripted day-to-day moments that sneak up on us, like dealing with a fool, struggling with wealth, or disciplining a child. Other kinds of moments occupy Proverbs, like those having to do with fairness, justice, integrity, self-discipline, family, a work ethic, moderation, humility, truthfulness, friendship, patience, guarding your mouth, letting go of control, living in the moment, not needing to be right—the little things that make up the successive moments of our lives.

It's a shame that talking about wisdom takes us into some abstract territory—like a life force or being with God at the beginning—but it is exactly wisdom like this that we need to live well in this unscripted, unpredictable, out-of-our-control, disordered existence of ours.

Think of it this way: the same wisdom that was with God when God "ordered" creation (Gen. 1) is available to us as we seek to "order" the chaos of our lives. When we seek and follow wisdom in the precious few years given to us, we are truly accepting a sacred responsibility to live intentionally in the Spirit's presence. And what that looks like will be different for each of us and will likely change through the seasons of our lives.

My midlife years brought up a lot of things that were off my radar in my twenties and thirties. I'm working on my stuff, and so are you, and that's the point—we are walking *our* paths, working through the unique moments of our lives and asking, "What does wisdom look like here and now?" We are doing our best to wing it well, by neither ignoring the Bible nor treating it as a recipe, but by accepting its invitation for something far better: living in the "energy" of the divine creative force, which is another way of saying the more familiar "living in the presence of God's Spirit."

Wisdom like that doesn't cultivate the worry and hand-wringing that so many experience about whether we can be absolutely sure we are doing the right thing in God's "perfect will." God's perfect will seems to be for us to seek and follow wisdom. This path is a serious one; it requires determination, discipline, humility, and vigilance and is hardly the comfortable and predictable way we might choose for ourselves. But it is not overbearing or burdensome. Wisdom, like a good parent, is patient and supportive, gives us freedom, and encourages and empowers us to work things out as best as we can.

To put it plainly, the life of faith *is* the pursuit of wisdom.

Think of the "stupid little thing" that last set you off, that got you unhinged, that decentered your soul and caused you pain. What was it? Maybe reading this book (ha-ha, I'm hilarious). An unfulfilled want. A harsh word you uttered. Pricked pride and offense taken. A worry over something you can't control.

Wisdom means to invade those nooks and crannies of our lives that we aren't even always aware of, the places our egos fight to keep hidden, the real us behind the facade we work so hard to prop up.

To live by faith—to live wisely—means living with an ever-increasing awareness of the hidden things, not simply a detached general knowledge that, say, "Money can be harmful," but a deep knowledge of *ourselves*, a true self-awareness of what money is doing *to me . . . right now.*

One of wisdom's great rewards is the true, raw, unfiltered, unchecked, honest knowledge of oneself. And this is anything but cheap self-help.

"Know thyself" might have been coined by Socrates and may sound like "secular" or "humanistic" advice, but it isn't. To gain honest knowledge of oneself is to see wisdom at work. In fact, one way of stating the goal of the life of faith is entering deeper and deeper into that kind of wisdom.

Show me a person of faith who knows herself well, and I will show you a true spiritual mentor—a truly wise person.

To skirt the difficult journey by using, of all things, the Bible as an impersonal one-size-fits-all list of dos and don'ts to shelter oneself in self-deception and a false sense of religious security blunts wisdom's sharp surgical edge.

Ironic, isn't it? What may appear to be the most biblical approach to the life of faith—"Do what the Bible says"—misses how the Bible actually works.

If we want a faith that is truly vibrant and active, we have to get used to the fact that God's presence comes not when we find the right passage, but when we embrace with courage—and anticipation—the way of wisdom.

* * *

We came to this point mainly (and not surprisingly) by way of the book of Proverbs, though already a few other portions of the Bible have crept in. And to sum up this entire chapter, wisdom is a really big deal in the Bible and if we miss it, we'll miss how the Bible actually works.

But now, we move to another part of the Bible to see wisdom at work—a part of the Bible that at first blush does indeed look like God's helicopter textbook. And yet even here wisdom reigns.

Especially here.

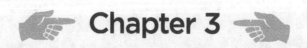

Chapter 3

God's Laws: Evasive and Fidgety Little Buggers

Some Details Would Be Nice, O Lord

If you've ever tried reading through the Bible daily from front to back, you may have noticed, besides the fact that it takes forever, that front-loaded are a lot of laws, 613 from what I understand (I never actually counted). After the book of Genesis, which is something of an extended introduction to the story of Israel, the next four books are largely taken up with commands of various sorts that God gave to Moses on Mt. Sinai, who dutifully relayed them to the Israelites waiting below.

These laws cover all sorts of scenarios concerning how Israelites are to treat each other and how they are to worship God. They are also, for many readers, hard to get through. You might find yourself wondering whether all this detail is really necessary, that God could really have stopped after the Ten Commandments and not gotten into leprosy, eating pork, or how to dress and ordain a priest. And so you move on to something that can hold your attention better, like the books of Joshua and Judges, in which—finally—people get impaled, have tent pegs driven into their heads, or are just generally dismembered. (Gather the kids and read out loud Joshua 10:26 and Judges 4:21 and 19:29.)

But here's the thing. Although we might not see the point of all these laws, God seems awfully intent on making sure the Israelites obey each and every one of them. Regardless of how *we* might scratch our heads about whether God actually cares about not using a chisel when building a stone altar or decoding exactly which four-legged insects we may eat, these commands aren't optional—which is what makes them commands.

In fact, penalties for disobeying some of these laws can get pretty severe, which in an uncomfortably large number of cases means being cut off from the group or executed. And not to pile it on, but Deuteronomy's warnings against disobedience get rather gruesome, including: drought, famine, blindness, having your children snatched away from you, and being forced to eat them because you're starving (see 27:11–28:68).

And yet, given their uncompromising and stern tone, biblical laws have a surprising quality: they tend to be ambiguous, which should be rather disconcerting given what is at stake.

When my family goes away for a few days and I ask someone to take care of our menagerie of dogs, cats, and rabbits (which at one point numbered as many as seven), I—the family administrator—leave instructions that could be used to illustrate one or more diagnoses in the DSM-V:

> In the morning the dogs need to go out between 6:00 and
> 8:00, depending on how late you let them out the night before.
> Give them each 1 cup of dry food mixed with 1½ tablespoons
> of wet food and a dash of water to create more gravy. Place
> the bowls on opposite sides of the kitchen, so they don't get

distracted. When you let them out, keep it to five minutes if you're not outside with them, but make it longer if you are, unless it's overly humid and/or hot. When they come in, they get a snack: the chicken treats in the morning, biscuits in the afternoon, and those teeth-cleaning things that look like toothbrushes in the evening. All three boxes are on the fridge, in order. Check their water twice a day and if it is less than half full, fill it.

Now, the cats. You'll notice two types of food on the shelf on the right side along the basement stairs . . .

People (namely my family) have told me I'm impossible to live with, but that's not on me. I won't—I *can't*—just say, "Please take care of our animals for us while we're gone, and be sure you do it right or you won't get paid!" and leave it at that. My holy commandments are clear and go on for two pages, single-spaced. After all, life on earth hangs in the balance. At least it does for the animals.

Likewise, when our children were younger and I ordered them from on high to clean their rooms or be banished to the Phantom Zone for all eternity, the *first* question I got was, "Whaddaya mean by 'clean'?" The stakes were high, and they wanted to know exactly what I expected of them. And if I complained about the crappy job they did, they read me the riot act about how I wasn't "clear" and it looked clean enough for them.

As odd as it might seem, most biblical laws really aren't clear. They may work as general guiding principles, sure, but when God says, "Thou shalt not," you're really hoping for some specifics.

But readers from ancient times have always understood that keeping a law means more than "doing what it says"; it means deliberating over what the command actually requires *here and now*.

Discerning how a law is to be obeyed, in other words, is an act of wisdom. Wisdom and Law,* as we will see, go hand in glove.

Pick most any law out of a hat—maybe something from the Ten Commandments. The Fourth Commandment says, *Remember the sabbath day, and keep it holy* (Exod. 20:8). Remembering the sabbath means to observe it, which means, as the following verses explain, to cease from all work (*sabbath* means "rest" or "cease" in Hebrew). This goes for all who live in the household, from the head on down to children and servants. Even the animals take a day off.

I suppose at first blush this seems clear enough. Just knock off the work one day a week as God said. How complicated could that be? Plenty complicated. For one thing, what *exactly* constitutes "work"?

In American Christian culture, not working might mean not going in on Sunday to that place that gives you a paycheck.** But is *work* only what we get paid for or is it any task that requires some exertion? Ancient Israelites didn't collect a paycheck, and yet they had this command to follow. What about cutting the grass, painting the trim, washing the car? And does it make any difference whether I might actually find cutting grass relaxing (I do)? Is it all relative? How do we know? Will God smite me for emptying the dishwasher or organizing my T-shirt drawer on a Sunday afternoon?

---

* Nerd note: *Law* is capitalized out of respect when referring to the body of laws in the Torah (or Pentateuch), the first five books of the Bible. Otherwise the lower case is used.

** The Christian sabbath (aka the Lord's Day) moved from the original Saturday of Judaism to Sunday as a celebration of Jesus's resurrection—unless you're a Seventh-Day Adventist and hold to Saturday. It's complicated. Which is more or less the point of this discussion.

And what if your Sunday leisure causes others to work? If you go to a movie or eat out, are you contributing to someone else's sin? It's easy to get paranoid. To be on the safe side you might just want to try standing still and practice shallow breathing for twenty-four hours.

And what about those of us who don't "go to work" in the conventional sense with clearly defined work hours? What if you're, say (hypothetically speaking, I'm asking for a friend), a college professor, who only teaches four hours a day, two days a week, but has to prepare whenever said hypothetical professor gets a chance, which usually involves reading, not to mention grading?

I can't get anything past you. I'm talking about me. Before we go on, please don't hate me because I have a great work schedule. Just remember that after college I went back to school for longer than a two-term presidency. And if we were to compare paystub-to-schooling ratios, you would have to agree I *deserve* this teaching schedule. And you can't take it from me.

But to make my point, reading is part of my job. Should I therefore not read on Sunday? Should I just play it safe and watch TV? Although someone has to find the remote (which I lost) and press the button. Is *that* work? And what do I do when a news ticker crosses my screen and I'm tempted to read it? Do I avert my eyes?

I'm getting ridiculous, I know. But more seriously we're not even getting into whether police, firefighters, surgeons, disaster-relief workers, or Apple customer service should have Sunday off—not to mention whether single mothers who need to feed their children and keep a roof over their heads can afford the luxury of "keeping the sabbath."

To complicate matters further (because that's what I do), although some Christians believe that observing the sabbath is still binding (because it's a "clear" biblical command), others argue that it's not, taking their cue from "clear" New Testament passages like Colossians 2:16–17 (sabbaths are a thing of the past) and Matthew 12:1–8 (Jesus himself "works" on the sabbath by plucking grain). So maybe for Christians sabbath keeping isn't a thing at all. It's really not clear either way, though that hardly keeps some Christians from almost coming to blows over it—and Calvinists know I'm only slightly kidding.

I'm not belittling sabbath keeping. I actually think the practice is spiritually and emotionally healthy, and I try to keep at least a different pace on Sunday, though I respect those who are more intense about it than I am. I'm only pointing out that how (or whether) to keep the command isn't clear.

No, this law isn't clear at all—even though in observing the day of rest the Israelites, at least according to the version in Exodus 20, are following God's own pattern set up in Genesis 1, where God created the world in six days and rested on the seventh. And in Deuteronomy 5, the motivation is different, but no less serious: since the Israelites were mistreated as slaves in Egypt, they must give their own slaves—and even animals—a day of rest.

There's a lot at stake here, but rather than clarity we get ambiguity. The law as written leaves its readers to ponder what it means and how to obey it here and now—in other words, to practice wisdom. Like it's on purpose.

Maybe You Didn't Hear Me: I Want Clarity

The challenge of keeping the sabbath command is only one example of a principle that holds for almost any law in the Old Testament, including the rest of the Ten Commandments. Here are all ten:

I. Don't worship other gods "before" Yahweh.*

II. Don't make idols.

III. Don't misuse God's name.

IV. Remember the sabbath day.

V. Honor your mother and father.

VI. Don't murder.

VII. Don't commit adultery.

VIII. Don't steal.

IX. Don't bear false witness.

X. Don't covet.

Pick any one of them and you'll hit some kind of ambiguity right away.

How do you know when you are actually misusing God's name? Is there a list of acceptable and unacceptable uses somewhere?** Can you say, "Oh my God, it's raining"? Is God even God's name or is it a title?

And what does it mean not to have other gods "before" Yahweh? Is there wiggle room? "Okay, Lord, no other gods *before* you. Got

---

* Yahweh is God's personal name in the Old Testament, though, truth be told, we're not sure that's correct. In Hebrew, all we have are four consonants, Y-H-W-H. The vowels are guesswork, though "Yahweh" is a respectable guess, thanks to a long history of linguists, who just *had* to know. But they don't really.

** To avoid the problem altogether, ancient Jewish scribes replaced the divine name Yahweh with *adonay* ("lord"). This practice is still reflected in modern English Bible translations, in which LORD (using small capitals instead of lowercase letters) replaces the divine name throughout.

it. But can I have one or two Canaanite gods *alongside* or perhaps tagging along *behind* you? You'd still be at the head of the line, of course."

On that last point, archaeologists have dug up hundreds of little clay figurines in the southern kingdom, Judah, dating to the seventh century BCE (the decades before the Babylonian exile). These figurines probably represent the Canaanite fertility goddess Asherah and were found in people's homes. Maybe they kept them on the mantle or nightstand.

The Bible takes a dim view of Israelites worshiping idols, and so we can be excused for thinking that all these figurines are just evidence of mass disobedience. But more likely the official view of Israel's religious leaders, which is what we read about in the Bible, didn't match the on-the-ground religious practices of the blue collar class. Judahite families of farmers and sheepherders might have thought, "Dang it all. My neighbor's crops are doing *great*, and they chalk it all up to Asherah, so maybe I should get on board. What's the harm? Yahweh is still first. He might even appreciate the company."*

Moving along, how exactly does one honor parents? Can they be questioned? Disobeyed—ever?

Can you kill in self-defense, to protect your family, when ISIS is invading your village, or when someone brings a semiautomatic rifle into a preschool?

Can you steal to save your child from starving? Someone else's child? And where is the line between coveting and admiration?

Strict legalism is a myth. Laws have a knack for ambiguity, and it

---

* Not to get sidetracked, but there is even archaeological evidence that some Israelites thought Asherah was Yahweh's wife. Another free piece of trivia for you.

only takes a moment of reflection to see that they have to be interpreted, which isn't exactly breaking news. The entire history of Judaism and Christianity bears witness to people of faith doing just that.

For me, though, a far more interesting question is lurking just below the surface. What are we to make of this ambiguity in, of all places, the Law beyond simply pointing out, "Hey, weird. That's really ambiguous"?

Biblical laws shout to us something about the Bible's purpose.

Even biblical laws, where one can't be faulted for expecting absolute crystal clarity, invite—even instigate—a lively discussion. When handled with a humble rather than anxious heart, laws drive us toward healthy community—not a tribalism geared toward insider-outsider thinking, but a community of faith where we can call upon wisdom as we deliberate and even debate how to live faithfully.

Laws are written in such a way to ensure that we can't just mindlessly tick off some boxes and call it "obedience." They might also prompt us to go to God directly with our questions and disagreement.

Parents who tell their twelve-year-old, "Clean your room, or no internet for a week," are just asking for a debate.

Maybe God is too.

Don't Forget Your PIN

Wisdom pushes her way front and center with virtually any law we look at. Right after the Ten Commandments in Exodus we come to several chapters (specifically 20:22–23:33) of laws collectively referred to as the Book of the Covenant (see 24:7; covenant being sort of a technical biblical term describing the legal relationship between God and the Israelites). These laws lay out what to do in various scenarios that the recently freed Hebrew slaves will encounter once they settle in the land of Canaan—such as laws covering the proper treatment of slaves, physical violence and injury, property, various matters of social justice, and other things.

We can almost put our finger down anywhere on these pages and ambiguity hits us like a blast of cold air:

> *Whoever strikes a person mortally shall be put to death. If it was not premeditated, but came about by an act of God, then I will appoint for you a place to which the killer may flee. But if someone willfully attacks and kills another by treachery, you shall take the killer from my altar for execution.* (Exod. 21:12–14)

I think a slick ancient Israelite criminal defense lawyer would have a field day here. How can you tell, really, if a violent act is actually premeditated and willful? You can make anything look like an accident, and violent offenders don't normally announce their treachery. And that "act of God" clause is just waiting to be exploited.

I am certain that the ancient Israelites knew as soon as the ink dried that these laws would need to be thought through, so that they could be *justly* and *fairly* administered. Wisdom, in other words, was not an add-on, but was always *central* for obeying any law in the Bible. Laws, once we begin thinking about what they mean and how they are to be obeyed, actually *push us to seek wisdom*, which goes beyond mechanical obedience.

It's not surprising, therefore, that ancient Jews came to think of wisdom and Law as inseparable—they need each other to work, like needing a pin number to access your cash.

In the second-century BCE book of Baruch (another book of the Old Testament Apocrypha), wisdom and Law are virtually equated: *Hear the **commandments** of life, O Israel; give ear, and learn **wisdom*** (3:9). Later wisdom is said to be immediately accessible to the people, not far away "in heaven" or "across the sea" (3:29–30). That's the exact same imagery used in Deuteronomy 30:12–13 to describe the *Law* (*It is not in heaven. . . . Neither is it beyond the sea*).

Another second-century book of the Apocrypha, Ecclesiasticus (or the Wisdom of Jesus Son of Sirach), takes an entire chapter to make the point (chapter 24). The author and revered sage Ben Sira praises wisdom in a manner reminiscent of the book of Proverbs: she, who was with God at creation, then comes to dwell in Jerusalem and grow like a *cedar in Lebanon*, inviting all to *eat* of her fruits—which means to learn to *work with* wisdom and *not sin* (24:13–22).

Ben Sira then slides effortlessly from wisdom to Law: *All this [the preceding lengthy description of wisdom] is the **book of the covenant** of the Most High God, **the law** that Moses commanded us as an inheritance for the congregations of Jacob* (24:23). Wisdom and Law seem virtually interchangeable.

But Ben Sira is not done. He goes on to tie the Law of Moses to a time long before Moses himself—to the creation story in Genesis, *as Proverbs does with wisdom*. Ben Sira writes that the Law *overflows* with wisdom (24:25), like the four rivers mentioned in Genesis 2:11–14 (the Pishon, Gihon, Tigris, and Euphrates) that flow from Eden to water the whole earth. Eventually, as Ben Sira puts it, the *water channel* becomes a *canal*, then a *river*, and finally a *sea* (24:30–31).

Ben Sira's point is that Law, not just wisdom, was there all along, flowing out from Paradise. We don't see this way of thinking in the Old Testament itself (at least not put so clearly), but now a few centuries later Ben Sira brings the Law back to the dawn of time, like wisdom, even though the Law does not actually appear until it is revealed to Moses on Mt. Sinai.

Ben Sira seems intent to show that Law, so central to Judaism, was not an afterthought during the time of Moses, but has been part of God's purpose for Israel all along—from the beginning. But why? Ben Sira may have thought such a move was needed, given the influence of Greek culture in his time, which threatened to undermine Jewish identity. And so Ben Sira made an adjustment to the biblical story of creation. Surely, Law was there from the beginning, just like wisdom.

Ben Sira's placing of the Law at the very beginning of the biblical story signals for us a central point of this book: *Changing times require adjustments to thinking about God and faith.*

We'll come back to that idea beginning in the next chapter and stay with it for a while, because getting that point right is huge for seeing how the Bible works.

* * *

Tying Law and wisdom together reflects what we've already seen: Law—however divine its origin and serious its requirements—is nevertheless ambiguous, and so "following the Law" and "seeking wisdom" are bound together for all time. Ancient Jews understood that following the commands *necessarily* took them beyond doing what the words said. Wisdom was needed to discern *how* to obey.

What a paradox. Even obedience to God is not scripted. Obedience is a wisdom exercise. Law without wisdom is incomplete.

And now we know why Judaism has such a long and rich tradition, often maligned and misunderstood by Christians, of deliberating over what exactly biblical laws require. Because these laws are ancient and ambiguous, Judaism has had no choice *but* to deliberate.

The Mishnah, the first major work of Jewish legal reflection (compiled around 200 CE), lists thirty-nine activities forbidden on the sabbath, including planting, plowing, cooking, sewing, slaughtering animals, and writing. This list may look like legalistic hand-wringing for some Christians, but it is actually *an exercise in wisdom* about discerning what work is in order to obey God.

Jewish tradition has always understood that keeping the sabbath law—and any law—means working out *how*. And that insight still holds for today as we too seek to know God in the pages of scripture.

Laws Don't Stand Still for Very Long

Not to start a fight, but here it goes. I'm not much of a fan of the NRA lobby. I say this with full knowledge that I will now lose their generous funding of my writing, but I need to speak my mind. It's not that I'm against guns, period. I just don't think that someone with an IQ of 70 and a documented history of violence should be able to pick up a military-grade bazooka at Toys-R-Us. Call me close-minded.

If you're still reading, let me get to my point. The Second Amendment to the US Constitution ("the right to keep and bear arms shall not be infringed") is sometimes understood to mean that government regulation of firearms *today* should be kept at a bare minimum. Now, I'm no Constitutional scholar, but I do have an internet connection, and I know that this 1791 amendment has had a long history of debate. The amendment itself arose in the wake of the Revolutionary

War to help ensure that a "well-regulated militia" could stand up against governmental oppression, should the new government decide to mimic the oppressive British one.

But the amendment made no provision for what to do when a militia is no longer needed, nor would we expect its framers to have a crystal ball. And they had no possible conception of firearms that could blast dozens of rounds in a few seconds and be operated by any primate with opposable thumbs, rather than muskets that have to be loaded one bullet at a time and actually require some skill to use.

Amendments are called amendments for a reason. Times change, and laws that made sense at one point in time don't necessarily make sense in another, and so they need to be amended. Some amendments themselves go out of date—the Third Amendment, concerning the quartering of soldiers in private homes, for example. And one amendment, the Eighteenth (prohibition), was famously repealed by another (the Twenty-First).

The point is that laws don't stay still. They can't. They're fidgety little buggers. Debating, amending, and even moving beyond some laws are part of the deal—and that includes the laws in the Bible.

We've already glimpsed that biblical laws are *ambiguous*—which means that how laws are kept is open to interpretation, and those interpretations reflect the circumstances of the interpreter. Laws are also *ancient*—they work in a world where, for example, slaves are less than fully human and virgin daughters are their father's property.* When we come across these laws, we need to either do some quick creative thinking or just move along and come back to them when

---

* Unfortunately, yes. Read Exodus 22:14–15 about making restitution for animals, then ignore that little subtitle most of your Bibles have, and go right to verses 16–17, which talk about virgins the same way. Exactly.

we have more energy. But we all know these laws present a problem: we just don't think like that anymore. Times have changed and what was law then is no longer law now.

And here's the thing: *we see this same dynamic in the Bible.*

Some laws were already outdated for later biblical writers. The Old Testament covers centuries of time, and as times and circumstances changed for the ancient Israelites, older laws sometimes had to be adjusted to speak God's word to new generations.

And that's one big reason why we see our third biblical characteristic, *diversity,* in the Old Testament laws—later biblical writers made adjustments to earlier laws, and both were kept in the Bible. For example . . .

Not to Beat a Dead Lamb, but . . .

Slavery is a horrible blight on the human drama, but in the ancient world—including the world of the Bible—it was as ordinary as today's blue-collar class. And laws were put in place about how to treat slaves in ways that passed for humane at the time.

Let me put it right out there that I think owning other human beings is wrong, even though the Bible assumes it's normal. Human slavery is one topic of the Bible for which wisdom clearly pushes us beyond the words on the page to accept the sacred responsibility to ask ourselves, "But what do *I* believe God is like? How does God want us to view our fellow humans today?"

It is clear from the book of Exodus that slaves were treated as property, not as full humans. The famous *eye for eye, tooth for tooth* law (Exod. 21:23–25) guarantees that justice will be fair in the event of physical injury, but not for slaves. If a slaveowner knocks out a slave's eye, he needs only to let the slave go, not lose an eye himself—the repercussions are merely economic.

A male Hebrew slave, however, has the option of going free after six years of service (along with his family, as long as he came in with one). No such choice is given to a female slave. Freedom can only be granted if she displeases her master (an ambiguous and unregulated idea) or if she is not properly provided for by her master, in which case she'd have to be bought back by her father. You can read all about this in Exodus 21:1–11.

The book of Deuteronomy, however, has a different take. Now both male and female Hebrew slaves may choose freedom after six years of service. Further, they are not to leave empty-handed. The slaveholder is instructed: *Provide liberally out of your flock, your threshing floor, and your wine press, thus giving to him some of the bounty with which the* Lord *your God has blessed you* (15:14).

This law is much nicer—let's call it more humane—and the motivation given for such treatment is Israel's own experience of being mistreated as slaves in Egypt (15:15). Sure, six years is still a long time, but that might have been the only way for some to get out of debt and survive. It's not a perfect system, and I'm happy to say that human civilization has come a long way. My point here, however, is that these two slave laws of Exodus and Deuteronomy don't match up, *even though they are both said to come from the same divine source*: God revealing his will to Moses on Mt. Sinai.

Let that sink in.

The book of Leviticus adds a third voice (25:39–47): *no* Hebrew is a slave, but a hired hand. In the "year of Jubilee" they all go free, no questions asked, because all Israelites are technically slaves of God, who brought them out of Egypt to serve him. Foreign slaves don't get this kind of treatment; they are still property.

Another example of diverse laws concerns the Passover meal, which commemorates Israel's exodus from Egyptian slavery. According to the book of Exodus, the meal is to be commemorated in the people's *houses* (12:3–4, 7, 19, 22) and consist of, among other things, a lamb *roasted* over fire—and most definitely not eaten raw or *boiled* (12:8–9). And this command is a *perpetual ordinance* for when they enter the land of Canaan eventually (12:24).

In Deuteronomy 16:1–9, however, we see no sign of this perpetual ordinance. Now the meal is to be held in *the place that the LORD will choose as a dwelling for his name* (verse 2), which is code in Deuteronomy for the Temple in Jerusalem. The family meal has become a national pilgrimage feast.

Deuteronomy also includes a somewhat stunning detail. Exodus is clear that the lamb is to be roasted over fire and *not to be boiled*. Deuteronomy, according to English translations, only says that the lamb is to be *cooked* (verse 7). So what's stunning about that? That word *cook* in Deuteronomy is the same Hebrew root word for *boil* in Exodus. In other words, the very thing not to be done in Exodus is commanded to be done in Deuteronomy without breaking stride.

Not to get off track, but the choice to translate the same Hebrew root word as *boil* in Exodus and *cook* in Deuteronomy is aimed at avoiding this contradiction. This isn't the only place this sort of thing tends to happen in modern translations of the Bible, though the better ones will provide helpful notes.

I certainly understand why translators might want to avoid a contradiction like this, but that motivation is coming from a Bible-as-rulebook mentality. Obscuring the tension between these two laws, besides causing readers to feel lied to when they later discover it, only creates obstacles for seeing how the Bible actually works as a wisdom book—where thinking about God and God's will changes over time.

And if that's not enough about food preparation, the book of 2 Chronicles has yet another take on the Passover law, and you have to hand it to this author for being ingenious. Apparently bothered by how God can give two different instructions for the same meal, this author fixes the problem by simply weaving the two together (35:13): the Passover *lamb* is to be *roasted* (as in Exodus) and the other *holy offerings* are to be *boiled* (as in Deuteronomy). And this writer is quick to point out that *this* Passover command follows the ancient ordinance. Indeed it does. Both of them.

The writer of 2 Chronicles, who lived long after the time of either Exodus or Deuteronomy, about two centuries after the return from exile, saw the contradiction and felt compelled to create a hybrid in order to resolve it. *Creative thinking about past laws is already happening during the biblical period.*

I don't want to beat a dead lamb, but let me say again that contradictions between Old Testament laws aren't exactly an industry secret. Jewish tradition has wrestled with them since before Christianity. Biblical scholars write books about it. Who knows, perhaps a future episode of *The Marvelous Mrs. Maisel* will have Midge's mom stressed out about how exactly to prepare the Passover lamb. For us, however, we really only need to note that the laws on slavery and the Passover differ, even though they are said to come from God on Mt. Sinai.

As startled as we might be at that notion, we are gaining here a pivotal insight. We are seeing wisdom at work—*rethinking older laws for new situations, bringing together the ancient and revered tradition with the ever-changing, real-life circumstances of God's people over time.*

In fact—and here's the interesting part—in order for these laws to remain God's word, they could *not* simply be left in the past, as an artifact of a bygone era. These laws had to be revisited and *adjusted* if future generations will also hear God's voice.

And I think I've just described the reality of what it means to "live biblically"—the wisdom act of bridging old and new.

Ambiguity in the Bible isn't a problem to be solved. It is a self-evident reality. It is also a gift, for this characteristic is precisely what allows the Law to be flexible enough to fit multiple situations over time. And, as I've been saying, it's not just we today who have to get creative; the ancient Jews already set the trajectory. They knowingly produced and embraced this wonderfully diverse and ambiguous collection of texts we call the Bible or Old Testament.

The Bible's very design gives us full permission to work out how to bridge the horizons of then and now for ourselves precisely *because* we too want to hear God's voice. But *how* those horizons are bridged is not the kind of information the Bible provides. That is where wisdom comes in.

Transposing the Past

The ancient, ambiguous, and diverse nature of the biblical laws are there for all to see, and Judaism and Christianity have had long and lively histories of debate about what to do with them.

And here is the absolutely vital and life-changing take-home point for us: *ancient* and *ambiguous laws*, in order to remain relevant, *needed* to be adapted—which results in the *diversity* of the laws we see in the Old Testament.

We can't miss what this is telling us today. Circumstances change, and *wisdom is needed to keep the divine–human conversation going.* Wisdom always shows up at the door anytime we read the Bible. That is how it has always been—and was meant to be.

Within the Bible itself we see writers both *respecting the past and transposing it to the present*—or better, they respect the past *by* transposing it, thus allowing the past to continue speaking. Transposing the past is an act of wisdom. It is not scripted. It can't be predicted. It just has to happen as it happens, in real time, by those seeking God's presence for their time.

Why would we think now, two to three thousand years later, that we somehow magically escape this biblically grounded process of transposing the past—that we, living in our postindustrialized, microchip-technologized, overstimulated world, would now be able to leave behind the process that even the ancient biblical authors could not: the need to rework the past, employing imagination and ingenuity, guided by the needs of the present?

Already for biblical writers, keeping the laws meant reengaging them when needed. And again, the genius of the laws *is* their ambiguity, not their clarity, for their ambiguity is the very thing that allows them to gain new life with each passing year, ensuring that past and present forever remain connected and in dialogue.

The Law cries out for wisdom. As we saw with Proverbs, what it means to keep a law here and now is as much a matter of "reading the moment" as it is reading the words on the page.

* * *

You might be asking yourself where I'm going with all this, and I wouldn't blame you. Yes, I tend to go on and on when I get excited about something, and I *am* excited about all this. We are seeing here vital clues about how the Bible works, what it is actually designed to do for us, which will open up to us the Bible as a book of wisdom that leads us toward wisdom.

And as for where all this is going, let's take a step back from the Law to glimpse other places where the Bible changes over time. And when we do that, we will be able to see even more clearly not simply *that* this sort of thing happens in the Bible, but *why*.

I've been circling around that question for a while now, and the answer is so straightforward you might wonder how you ever missed it.

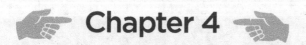

Chapter 4

Wisdom =
Time + Diversity

Changing the Script

My wife, Sue, and I raised three amazing* children, who have some-how managed to become semifunctioning adults with less than oppressive college debt and no significant brushes with the law. In other words, on the Enns family intergenerational scale of emotional health, they are psychological triumphs.

I wasn't perfect as a father, as I'm sure you've already concluded. I made mistakes, but I also learned a lot as time went by—like the fact that, though there are general guidelines for how to parent well (lock up the cleaning products, don't give your two-year-old a knife, Smarties are not a food group), no parenting script can take you from birth to adulthood. It usually can't get you past lunch.

Or, perhaps better, we write the script as we go, in tune with the moment, and subjecting that script to constant revision simply as a matter of survival and sanity. Parents have to stay flexible and be ready to adjust on the fly, because situations change and children get older.

I really can't think of a better analogy for how the Bible works as a wisdom book. And I do mean the Bible as a whole.

---

* (Are you still reading this, guys?! Again, PLEASE don't put me in a home.)

We've already seen how Proverbs, with its baked-in antiquity, ambiguity, and diversity, is designed to funnel us toward wisdom, so we can tap into the life force of the cosmos and learn to live wisely amid the unexpected twists and turns of life. We saw that even the Law, which we might think would be God's heavenly helicopter-parenting book, is nothing of the sort, but likewise pushes us toward wisdom. Otherwise the laws would stay locked in the past.

A Bible that does things like this is not a disappointing problem that has to be explained away or made excuses for, but something to be embraced with thanksgiving as a divine gift of love, as we, in return, accept our sacred and biblical responsibility to walk daily the path of wisdom rather than looking to hitch an easy ride.

But now I want to narrow our focus to something we've only glimpsed thus far. *The Bible's diversity is the key to uncovering the Bible's true purpose for us.*

Different voices coexist in the Bible, because the Bible records how writers in their day and in their own way dealt with the antiquity and ambiguity of their sacred tradition.

It's not enough for us simply to observe *that* diversity exists. We need to understand more clearly *why*. And because this is going to be such a big deal from here on out, let me repeat: *The diversity we see in the Bible reflects the inevitably changing circumstances of the biblical writers across the centuries as they grappled with their sacred yet ancient and ambiguous tradition.* And again, the same could be said of people of faith today.

We don't see *this* type of diversity *over time* in Proverbs. Yes, Proverbs says different things about wealth, as we've seen, but those sayings aren't different *because* they were written at different points on Israel's historical timeline. Some sayings might have had earlier oral precursors, but given their general nature, there is no way to date these sayings; they could just as easily all have been written by one sage on one day.

The Law, however, is tied to a storyline, and so, as we've seen, laws in Deuteronomy and Exodus differ, because they are separated on Israel's timeline by wandering and soul-searching in the desert for forty years (at least as the story is told—hold that thought). Deuteronomy adapted and adjusted earlier laws for later times and circumstances, like amendments to the Constitution or a Supreme Court ruling that the Second Amendment allows the banning assault rifles, because the world has changed since the eighteenth century.

What is true of the Law is also true of the Bible generally. *The Bible (both Old and New Testaments) exhibits this same characteristic of the sacred past being changed, adapted, rethought, and rewritten by people of faith*, not because they disrespected the past, but because they respected it so much they *had* to tie it to their present.

I'll go even farther. Without such changes over time, Christianity wouldn't exist. The Christian tradition *depends* on these changes over time—and some rather big ones at that. But we'll leave that for later. For now it's enough to say,

The Bible isn't a book that reflects one point of view. It is a collection of books that records a conversation—even a debate—over time.

When I began to see that for myself, a lot of things fell into place about the Bible's purpose and what it means to read it with the eyes of faith. When we accept the Bible as the moving, changing, adaptive organism it is, we will more readily accept our own sacred responsibility to engage the ancient biblical story with wisdom, to converse with the past rather than mimic it—which is to follow the very pattern laid out in the Bible itself.

A rulebook view of the Bible misses that dynamic process entirely; indeed, it seems determined to obscure it.

The Most Important Part of the Book Thus Far

Thinking of the Bible as shifting and moving may feel spiritually risky, bordering on heretical, but it isn't. Sermons, Bible study materials, prayer books, and the like adapt the ancient words for modern benefit all the time. Biblical psalms that praise the Lord and then ask God to squash the enemy are often edited for church consumption. Generally speaking, Christians think asking God to kill their enemies is wrong (Jesus said so), so adjustments are made to those parts of the Bible that say exactly that. Laws that assume the legitimacy of slavery or virgins as their fathers' property are omitted or given a more spiritual spin. The list goes on.

None of these modern adaptations is "in the Bible," and yet even the most committed "rulebook Bible" readers out there wind up adapting what the Bible says, because we have to—if we want that ancient text to continue to speak to us today.

And what is true of us is already true of the biblical writers. Between the earliest writings of the Old Testament (around 1200 BCE) and the latest writings of the New (around 100 CE), about thirteen hundred years passed.* The last biblical writers were as far removed from the first as we today are removed from the invention of gunpowder and the rule of Charlemagne. The idea that every writer over that great span of time was on the same page at every moment in spite of the myriad of complex and changing social and political factors is hard to accept in theory and impossible to accept when we read the Bible and see the diversity for ourselves.

Adaptation over time is baked thoroughly into the pages of *the Bible as a whole* and as such demonstrates that the Bible is a book of wisdom, demanding to be adapted again and again by people of faith living in vastly distant cultures and eras—including our own, removed by as much as two millennia from the time of its completion.

And so, to repeat an earlier point, if the ancient biblical writers themselves needed to make adjustments about how they were hearing God speaking to them, whatever would make us think that we can escape that same process? Indeed, if we, like the biblical writers, want to stay connected to that past, why would we even want to try to escape?

When, where, and under what circumstances they lived all affected how the biblical writers perceived God, their world, and their place in it. The same holds for us. The moments of time, place, and location we occupy cannot help but play a major role in shaping how we understand God and the life of faith.

---

* Because I know someone is going to ask, here is another nerd note. Although it may be best to keep an open mind, most biblical scholars conclude that the earliest portions of the Old Testament are snippets that stem from about the thirteenth century BCE and include old poems such as Exodus 15 and Judges 5. The latest written was Daniel in the second century BCE. The earliest New Testament writings may be as early as the late 40s CE (1 Thessalonians) and the latest around the 90s CE (Revelation, the Gospel of John, the Pastoral Letters), if not later. Acts and 2 Peter may have been later still.

And, as I've been saying, that reshaping is an act of wisdom. We have to work it through and figure it out.

In *that* sense, one can speak of the Bible as "timeless"—not because its commands and teachings remain fixed and impervious to change, but because they are clearly not. Without its unwavering commitment to adaptation over time, the Bible would have died a quick death over two thousand years ago. Its existence as a source of spiritual truth that transcends specific times and places is made possible by its flexibility and adaptive nature—one of the many paradoxes we need to embrace when it comes to the Bible.

The biblical writers were human like us, and nothing is gained by thinking otherwise. Someone might say, "Well, okay, sure they were human, obviously, but the biblical writers were also *inspired*, directed by God in what to write, and so not simply ordinary human writers." I get the point. To see the Bible as inspired by God is certainly the mainstream view in the history of Christianity (and Judaism), but what that means exactly and how it works out in detail have proved to be quite tough nuts to crack.

Answers abound (and conflict) and no one has cracked the code, including me. But any explanation of what it means for God to inspire human beings to write things down would need to account for the diverse (not to mention ancient and ambiguous) Bible we have before us. Any explanation that needs to minimize, cover up, or push these self-evident biblical characteristics aside isn't really an explanation; it's propaganda.

Okay, I'm getting a little negative about this. Sorry. It's just that there was a time when I was also very keen to work out some abstract theory about God's role in producing the Bible, but that task no longer interests me. I've learned—by reading the Bible again and again—to accept and be grateful for this messy Bible we have, which drives us, as I've been saying, away from thinking of it as a stagnant pond of rules and regulations and toward thinking of it as a flowing stream that invites us to step in and be refreshed anew every day in following Jesus here and now.

Biblical writers living in different times and places who wrote for different reasons and under different circumstances have modeled for us the centrality of wisdom for the life of faith. To rethink the past in light of the present moment, as the ancient writers did, is—again—not an act of faithlessness, but the very thing faith demands. To do what is necessary to bring the past to meet the present is the highest sign of respect. A wooden, inflexible view of the Bible doesn't allow that.

Some of us might understandably bristle in the quiet of our hearts at such an idea. And that's okay. Take your time. My aim here is not to force anyone to stop bristling, but to point out that the biblical writers didn't bristle. For them, a life of faith and of rethinking the content of that faith weren't at odds with one another, but worked off of each other. The ancient Jews understood full well that an authoritative tradition cannot simply stay in the past and still have its say. It must be brought into the present to speak to the present.

The ancient Jewish scribes living in the centuries after the return from exile (after 539 BCE) were responsible for collecting these ancient traditions into one book (the Jewish Bible or Christian Old Testament). They clearly valued this centuries-long process of bringing the past and present into conversation. They intentionally included all this diversity in their editing work rather than snuffing it out.

They were wise. They already knew that honoring this "trajectory of change" was the only way to stay connected to the past as they lived in their present and hoped for their future.

The Bible shows us that obedience to God is not about cutting and pasting the Bible over our lives, but seeking the path of wisdom—holding the sacred book in one hand and ourselves, our communities of faith, and our world in the other in order to discern how the God of old is present here and now. We respect the Bible best when we take that process seriously enough to own it for ourselves—but that is getting ahead of things a bit.

First, let's take a deeper look—though still only a glimpse—at how daringly some biblical writers adapted the past to let God speak in the present. And to do that, we need to loop back to Deuteronomy for a moment.

This Part Is So Exciting!

According to the biblical timeline, Deuteronomy and Exodus are separated by forty years of wilderness wandering, but the actual distance between them is much greater. And to see that we need to dip one or two toes into the exciting, star-studded, never boring, sexy, and lucrative world of biblical scholarship.

For various reasons, biblical scholars for over two hundred years have argued—persuasively—that Deuteronomy was written much more than forty years after Moses's time (generally understood to be about 1300 BCE). Actually, that isn't just a modern theory, but goes back to the early centuries of Christianity, at least as far back (from what I can tell) as the church father Jerome, who lived around the year 400 CE. He mused that someone long after Moses, probably Ezra—who lived in the fifth century BCE—had possibly touched up Deuteronomy.

Jerome's observation is probably something of a passing comment, a side hunch, to explain some peculiarities of Deuteronomy. But fast-forward a few centuries, and we find modern scholars working through Deuteronomy systematically and proposing more detailed arguments for how and when Deuteronomy came to be. Some of those arguments can get fairly nuanced, and for our purposes here we can safely sidestep all of that.* We just need to see that the main reasons for dating Deuteronomy much later than Moses's time come from Deuteronomy itself.

For example, Deuteronomy begins, *These are the words Moses spoke to all Israel beyond [on the other side of] the Jordan*. Notice that the writer here is talking *about* Moses, and so the writer isn't Moses himself. Also, Moses is not said to do any writing; he speaks, but he does not write. Although a historical Moses's words may be the basis for the book (though that is far from certain), the writer of Deuteronomy clearly created the book itself.

Also, Deuteronomy tells us that Moses died *in the land of Moab* (34:5) and never crossed the Jordan River to enter Canaan with the rest of the Israelites—it's sort of a big deal that Moses of all people never entered the promised land. So, since the writer refers to the words Moses spoke "on the other side of the Jordan," we know that means the writer is standing on the side of the Jordan that Moses never set foot on. The writer isn't Moses.

---

* For those of you who hate sidestepping, the Wikipedia article on the "Book of Deuteronomy" does a great job explaining all this: https://en.wikipedia.org/wiki/Book_of _Deuteronomy#cite_note-3.

Already in the first verse, the anonymous writer isn't exactly trying to hide the fact that someone after Moses wrote the book. But how long after Moses?

Assigning dates to books of the Bible is tricky, and the best arguments are also quite nerdy and long (don't tempt me). Still, Deuteronomy itself gives us some signs that a lot of time had passed from the time of Moses to the author's day.

First, after notice of Moses's death in the last chapter of Deuteronomy, we are told that *no one knows his burial place to this day* (34:6). Unless the Israelites had immediate mass memory loss, "to this day" surely suggests (as it did to Jerome*) that a lot of time had passed—so much time, in fact, that the grave site of the most important person in the Old Testament is unknown.

Second, just below in verse 10, we read, *Never since has there arisen a prophet in Israel like Moses.* This comment—no one has *ever* come close to Moses—is actually stripped of its power unless a long time had passed.

One more example (of many) comes from Deuteronomy 4:37–38. Moses—who never entered the promised land—speaks of the possession of the promised land as a *present* reality: *He [God] brought you out of Egypt with his own presence, by his great power, driving out before you nations greater and mightier than yourselves, to bring you in, giving you their land for a possession, **as it is still today**.*

As it is still today indicates that whoever wrote this was living

---

* To quote Jerome, "We must certainly understand 'this day' as meaning the time of composition of the history, whether one prefers the view that Moses was the author of the Pentateuch or that Ezra reedited it. In either case I make no objection" (*The Perpetual Virginity of Blessed Mary* 7). Jerome's casual tone suggests that the problem of Deuteronomy 34:6 was already well known in his day.

in the land of Canaan long after Moses, after God had driven the Canaanites out of the land and given the land to the Israelites. Most scholars have concluded that this was written after the establishment of the monarchy—no earlier than 1000 BCE, and likely, for other reasons, centuries later.

We could go on, but I'm not writing a book on Deuteronomy. I only want to point out that Deuteronomy was written from a much later point of view than Exodus. When exactly was Deuteronomy written? The broad consensus is in the latter half of the seventh century BCE based on an earlier (perhaps eighth-century) prototype and then subject to revisions up to and including the time of the Babylonian exile and perhaps later.

More specifically, scholars generally agree that Deuteronomy reflects a particular moment in Israel's history—the Assyrian threat to the southern kingdom, Judah, in the seventh century BCE, after the deportation of the northern kingdom by the Assyrians in 722 BCE. In fact, Deuteronomy as a whole is structured like the treaties the Assyrians made with their conquered foes.

That's why the book as a whole is structured like Assyrian treaties, which begin with an overview of the sovereign's great deeds (Deut. 1–4), followed by the stipulations of the treaty (the laws, Deut. 5–26), and the promise of blessings for obedience and curses for disobedience with both parties bearing witness (Deut. 27–28). As we glimpsed earlier, the laws of Deuteronomy in particular differ in places from those in Exodus (and Leviticus), because they are set at a different time and under different circumstances. The command to celebrate the Passover meal in the Temple (not in the people's houses) reflects the central importance of the Temple as the national political and religious symbol of God's presence.

The overall message of Deuteronomy is that the people of Judah are to make an alliance only with their true King, Yahweh, and not with the Assyrians, despite the great threat. In other words, be faithful to Yahweh; trust him alone. And Deuteronomy is the treaty.

I swear on my heart that this is so interesting, which is why I got into this line of work and needed to take out a home-equity loan to marry off my daughter and reshingle my roof. But I'm not dragging you through all this to justify my sorry existence. The bottom line is that Deuteronomy is a late revision of ancient law. And what is so striking and so vital in all of this is that whoever was responsible for Deuteronomy apparently had no hesitation whatsoever in updating older laws for new situations and *still calling it the words that God spoke back then to Moses on Mt. Sinai* (or Horeb, as it is called in Deuteronomy), even though they don't match what God said in Exodus.

This writer wasn't an idiot. He knew *exactly* that his words differed. But by saying that *his* words were the ones spoken by God to Moses a generation earlier, he was making a huge spiritual claim that we simply cannot miss and should take to heart: *The writer of Deuteronomy sees his updating of the older laws as God's words for his time and place.*

And so God isn't just a voice out of the past. God still speaks.

You Were There

One truly remarkable passage, Deuteronomy 5:1–5, illustrates this point, and I can't tell you how many times I read this before I finally saw it. Moses relays the Ten Commandments to this new generation of Israelites living forty years after these commandments were first given on Mt. Horeb (Sinai), and he says:

> *Hear, O Israel, the statutes and ordinances that I am addressing to you today; you shall learn them and observe them diligently. The LORD our God made a covenant **with us** at Horeb. **Not with our ancestors** did the LORD make this covenant, **but with us, who are all of us here alive today**. The LORD spoke **with you** face to face at the mountain, out of the fire. (At that time I was standing between the LORD and you to declare **to you** the words of the LORD; for **you were afraid** because of the fire and did not go up the mountain.)*

"With us . . . with us . . . with you . . . to you." How can that be? The whole point of the forty-year time-out between Sinai and Moab was for the disobedient original generation to die in the wilderness, so God could start over again with a new batch of Israelites. So why is this writer treating this new generation as if they were present forty years ago when by definition they weren't? This makes no sense.

Or does it?

Think of Deuteronomy as a motivational sermon. *The second generation was to see itself as the "exodus generation," to whom God is present and accessible, not a long-gone deity from days of old.*

Deuteronomy *reimagines* God for a new time and place. Deuteronomy is, in other words, an act of wisdom. For the past to have any spiritual vitality *in* the present, it had to be reshaped *for* the present.

Reimagining God. We'll be coming back to that idea a lot from here on out.

This practice of making the exodus present has continued throughout Jewish history in the Passover seder—all Jews everywhere are to see themselves as the exodus generation, saved by God.

I won't lie. Deuteronomy is a hard book to wrap our heads around and drives scholars batty. But it is also a beautiful book for showing us how *the Bible itself* models that God keeps speaking, that God is not just a God of the past, but a God of the present—and we are truly responsible people of faith when we keep our eyes and ears open for how, reading the times as well as the text.

If such a view of the Bible alarms or concerns us, it may be because we are harboring a false expectation of the Bible as a source of unchanging information, an expectation the Bible seems designed to dismiss.

Deuteronomy doesn't line up with Exodus not because the writer was distracted and dropped the ball, but because Deuteronomy is an act of wisdom. The author accepted the sacred responsibility to rethink the past because the changing circumstances demanded it: "What does God require today? How do we embody God here and now, in our time?"

When we miss how the book of Deuteronomy works, we miss a great opportunity to see how the Bible can and *must* also work for us—as a sacred text to be taken seriously that also impresses upon us the responsibility of going beyond it. Deuteronomy gives us permission to strike out in bold faith to discern what it means to live God's way for our time—not by scripting that for us but by modeling for us a process that we now have to own for ourselves. And thus the Bible, rather than closing down the future, sets us on a journey of relying on God's presence to discover it.

It is much maligned in some Christian circles to suggest that different times require different responses, since "The Bible is God's word. People may change, but God never changes." I understand the logic, but the author of Deuteronomy doesn't agree.

Neither does the prophet Ezekiel.

Peel Me a Sour Grape of Wrath

Like the author of Deuteronomy, the prophet Ezekiel lived around the time of the Babylonian exile. A prophet's job in the Bible was to interpret for the people the events of the day from God's point of view—in Ezekiel's case, to proclaim that the sack of Jerusalem and the (for all intents and purposes) end of the nation of Judah was no accident of history, but God's punishment for generations of corruption, namely, worshiping false gods.

This, of course, was bad news, but that's what prophets did. They never showed up just to say, "Hey, everyone. I just wanted to stop by and say you're doing *great*! Keep it up." Prophets delivered bad news—also now and then with a ray of hope—but generally speaking they weren't the perky life-of-the-party kinds of folk you want to hang out with. Definitely not the type of people you ask to come speak at the church fund-raiser.

Having said that, in Ezekiel 18 we find a turn for the better. It seems that God has heard a complaint and has sent his prophet to clear things up.

Apparently, a saying was making the rounds at the time: *The parents have eaten sour grapes, and the children's teeth are set on edge*

(18:2). As the following verses make clear, this saying is a complaint: children are exiled in Babylon for what their parents did (worshiping foreign gods). If the *parents* were the ones who ate the sour grapes, why should the *children's* teeth be *on edge*? Think of how your jaw locks when you bite into a lemon. Pretty effective metaphor, if you ask me.

Anyway, that doesn't seem fair, does it? No, it doesn't. Not one bit.

One can easily imagine that some of the deported Judahites were too young to have actually done anything all that wrong. And, if you think about it for a second, plenty of deportees were probably not themselves serious offenders but just got caught up in the mayhem. Still others were born in captivity and weren't even alive when the wrongs were done.

So why are all these people being punished by this prolonged time-out when they themselves didn't do anything to deserve it? Why are their teeth on edge? And if this is how God operates, maybe God isn't just at all!

Ezekiel's answer—better, *God's* answer spoken through Ezekiel—is: *As I live, says the LORD God, this proverb shall **no more** be used by you in Israel. Know that all lives are mine; the life of the parent as well as the life of the child is mine; **it is only the person who sins that shall die*** (18:3–4).

It's as if God is saying, "Yes, I see your point."

Ezekiel goes on for a few paragraphs laying out various scenarios to make it absolutely clear what God means. God will bless a righteous and lawful man, but if his son is wicked, that son will be treated as he deserves; he can't appeal to his father's reputation. Likewise, if the son is righteous and does not follow in his father's wicked footsteps, he will not bear his father's punishment.

There's more to it, but we get the gist: everyone is treated by God as they deserve. The son doesn't get a free pass because dad was the model of obedience, nor is the father's punishment for wickedness downloaded onto the son.

Okay, why bring this up at all? Because the exiled Judahites were struggling with God's fairness —wasting away in a foreign land, punished by God for something some of them had no part in, wondering whether all this God business was really worth the effort. If God's justice looks like this, we might be better off giving up on being Israelite and instead joining a softball league or community theater.

And so God declares the promise that everyone will be treated as *they* deserve.

Of course, this is wonderful, but here's the problem. Ezekiel's prophecy, his word from the Lord, collides with an earlier word from the same Lord—the Second Commandment, against false worship (the making of idols).

In Exodus 20:4–6 (and the later version in Deut. 5:8–10), false worship merited a punishment extending *to the third and the fourth generation.** The blessings for obedience will linger *to the thousandth generation*. Sure, that's a bit of an exaggeration, which the Bible tends to do a lot when numbers are involved, but the point still sticks: when it comes to worshiping God, obedience and disobedience have multigenerational effects: children *are* blessed or punished for what their parents did.

Remember that *the* sin that landed the Judahites in exile wasn't something like stealing or adultery or murder, but the very same

---

* No need to expect literal information from that number, but it matches roughly the length of the Babylonian exile.

topic that occupies the Second Commandment, false worship, which had been sponsored by one dumb Judahite king after another.

It's hard to miss the implication of Ezekiel's words: *God clearly said one thing to Moses in the Second Commandment at the beginning of Israel's journey, and then God clearly says something different through Ezekiel at the end.*

Briefly, another example of diversity in the Bible over time is found in the story of King Jehu's bloody coup in 2 Kings 9–10, a story from the days of the divided monarchy. In that definitely not-for-children's story, Jehu is anointed by the prophet Elisha to hurry on to Jezreel and massacre the entire royal family of wicked king Ahab, including seventy of his sons. Thus began the dynasty of Jehu, and it all happened *according to the word of the LORD that he spoke to Elijah* earlier in 2 Kings 10:17.

But another prophet, Hosea, seems to have taken issue with this coup—or better, according to Hosea, *God takes issue with it.*

> *In a little while I will punish the house of Jehu for the blood of Jezreel, and I will put an end to the kingdom of the house of Israel. On that day I will break the bow of Israel in the valley of Jezreel.* (Hos. 1:4–5)

So, which is it? How does God feel about Jehu's coup? It depends on which book of the Bible you're reading. These two authors give polar opposite perspectives on Jehu's act.

To explore why exactly these two authors handle Jehu's coup in opposite ways is a very interesting topic, but ultimately speculative. Let's not get into all that. My point is simply that the Bible does this sort of thing, and when it does, we need to see it not as a problem, but an invitation. These scenes crack open for us a window onto a different way of experiencing God through the Bible. The circumstances of Ezekiel and Hosea's days required a different "word from the Lord" than what had been in effect earlier.

Does this mean God changes? I don't think so (though some do*). It means, rather, as I see it, that different times and different circumstances call for people of faith to perceive God and God's ways differently.

God doesn't change, but God—being God—is never fully captured by our perceptions. As people continue to live and breathe and experience life, how they see God changes too.

I'm sure as a parent I've said to one or more of my children, "Watch what you do, because the habits you form now will stay with you for life and even be passed down to your own children without your even knowing it." In fact, I can vouch for that as a parent—tendencies I picked up from my parents were downloaded onto my children, and I didn't even realize it until they were in their teens.

But then at other times, like after a discouraging failure, I might say, "Don't worry. Your life script isn't written by this one moment. Tomorrow's another day, and you can always start afresh."

These are two separate parenting moments that require a different word. The same holds for clergy when caring for people—the moment, not the rulebook, dictates the words spoken. It takes *wisdom* to

---

* Process theologians and openness theologians say that God does change. Frankly, that topic is above my paygrade.

know what to say in what situation, because different situations call for different types of pastoral responses.

So why can't the biblical writers, and God who is somehow mysteriously behind them, do the very same thing? I think they can, and in fact they do—especially when in crisis mode. And speaking of which . . .

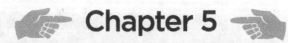

Chapter 5

When Everything Changes

Rachel Is Weeping for Her Children

I'm a father of three adult children. Adult. I don't take that for granted.

No joke here. When my children were young, a lurking fear was that something would happen to them. The rash of child abductions that flooded the news in the late 1980s and early 1990s gave me a lot of anxiety, which I more or less kept to myself.

The closest we got to realizing this fear was one day at the mall. We were about to walk out of a store, and all of a sudden our two-year-old wasn't there. We scanned the store quickly. No sign. I barked orders: "Sue, you go through the store. I'll stand at the entrance and scan the mall up and down." In an instant I uttered every stock prayer I knew, including the "Oh Lord, if you bring her back to us, I promise to . . ." prayer.

We found her thirty seconds later (or was it thirty hours?) playing under a dress rack. I was shaken for days.

I cannot imagine losing a child. And I do not say this lightly, because I know people who have. Losing a child, for whatever reason, shapes your life narrative from there on out. It will be *the* reference point of the past, the time when everything tragically changed and the deepest possible questions of faith became your constant companion—like, as one mother said to me years ago, "Where the f*** was God when my son was killed?"

I trust no one will misunderstand my intentions. I don't mean to compare the loss of a child to anything, let alone a national tragedy that happened a distant twenty-six hundred years ago. But I also know modern Western Christians have a lot of trouble identifying with the depth of panic and pain of the Babylonian exile, which one prophet compared to a mother losing her children:

> *Thus says the LORD:*
>
> *A voice is heard in Ramah,*
> *lamentation and bitter weeping.*
>
> *Rachel is weeping for her children;*
> *she refuses to be comforted for her children,*
> *because they are no more.* (Jer. 31:15)

Rachel, the wife of Jacob in Genesis, is here symbolized as the "national mother," disconsolate, watching as her children, vulnerable and defenseless, are plundered and pillaged and then taken a thousand miles away to Babylon. Surely, these children are *no more*.

Exile was *the* trauma of the Old Testament—and we dare not underestimate its impact.

Moving to Babylon wasn't just a setback, an inconvenience. The Israelites believed they owed their existence to God's irrevocable promise to Abraham of countless descendants and a perpetual kingdom of their own in a land of their own—the land of Canaan (Gen. 12, 15). That promise was confirmed throughout Israel's story in a series of steps, beginning with the miraculous birth of Abraham's son Isaac (Gen. 17), Israel's deliverance from Egyptian slavery and receiving the Law on Mt. Sinai (Exodus, Leviticus), the successful conquest of Canaan (Joshua), and the founding of the monarchy with God's chosen king, David, on the throne (1–2 Samuel). Through all these stages, the Israelites had their share of rebellions and murmurings against God, and things rarely went as planned. But still, God stuck with them. God had made a promise after all.

The first major crisis came when God took the nation of Israel from David's grandson Rehoboam and divided it into the northern and southern kingdoms (around 930 BCE). The causes were Solomon's introduction of false worship into Israel (due to the influence of his many foreign wives), and Rehoboam's very shortsighted and undiplomatic handling of a volatile political moment (see 1 Kings 11–12). The northern kingdom eventually fell to the Assyrians in 722 BCE, leaving only the rump state of Judah to the south. And so the bulk of the promised land was no longer in Israelite possession, and the chosen people in the north were never heard from again.

The ancient promises were beginning to unravel. But at least there remained a remnant, the nation of Judah.

But imagine if an invading army took control of the western two-thirds of the continental United States, deported many of its residents to South America, and erased state lines, leaving intact only the states east of the Mississippi River? Sure, we can see an upside (do we really need Texas and *two* Dakotas?), but the drastic change would be rather traumatic nonetheless and result in a lot of soul searching about what it means to be an American—especially if you believe this is God's country (which it isn't, but that's another book).

But the worst was yet to come. In 586 BCE,* after a decade of struggle, the mighty Babylonians under their dreaded king, Nebuchadnezzar, exiled a portion of the southern kingdom after destroying Jerusalem and burning the Temple to the ground.

The Temple, mind you. God's dwelling place.

Now the chosen people have no land, no king, and no Temple. That's just another way of saying that God has abandoned them.

The exile is Judah's tragic story, *the* reference point of the past, that moment that would now color all others and that needed to be processed:

> How could God let this happen?
>
> How could God abandon us?
>
> How could God turn his back on a promise that goes back to Abraham?
>
> What will happen to us now?
>
> Are we no longer the chosen people?

The people of Judah did return from Babylonian captivity in 538 BCE,** due to the policy of the conquering Persians of resettling the peoples that the Babylonians had deported. So that's good news. But the Persian Empire did rule over the land of Judah for the next two hundred years, and during that time the questions shifted a bit:

---

* The date is either 586 or 587. It was a long time ago and a year either way is close enough.

** Or 539. I hope you're not losing sleep over these dates. They should make you feel smarter, actually. If you're in a Bible study and some know-it-all shows off by throwing out "538," you can say, "Or 539. Scholars give both dates." But only if you sense this is the time to "answer a fool."

How much *longer* before we have our own king again?

When will things *finally* get fully back to normal?

What do we do in the *meantime*?

Yes, the Judahites were in a full-blown, centuries-long crisis that would come to lodge itself deeply in the Jewish consciousness. And that crisis would have to be processed, so the Judahites did what anyone would have done under the circumstances—they told *their* story:

> This is who we are.
>
> This is where we came from.
>
> This is what we believe of God.
>
> This is where things went wrong.
>
> This is our hope for a renewed future.

Christians call that story the Old Testament.

Don't we too sooner or later want to tell our story when faced with tragedies and hardships? We need to give our crisis a narrative, something to tell ourselves and others so we can make some sense of the pain and find hope for tomorrow. We may tell our story to a friend over coffee or on a blog. We might journal—or even write a book or two. And the Judahites, in the centuries following the return from Babylon, created what would come to be called the Jewish Bible or Christian Old Testament.

I don't mean to suggest that nothing had been written down until this sixth-century national crisis of faith. Certainly the Israelites long before had written stories, accounts of battles, court records of kings, and poems and songs to express who they were, where they came from, and how their God, Yahweh, is wrapped up in all of it. But it was only in the wake of the crisis of God's abandonment that they *needed* to tell their *whole* story—to make sense of how broken their past had been and how shattered it had become as they "wept by the waters of Babylon" (as Ps. 137 puts it).

Without the crisis of exile, the Bible as we know it wouldn't exist.

We've lingered here in the exile for a few pages, because it is *the* changing circumstance that brought the ancient Judahites to their knees and forced them to engage their past and *reimagine God for their present and future.* The ancient Judahites, who would later come to be called Jews, *had* to tell their story. They had to account for the crisis, to process it, and to move forward to a better future.

That's how the Bible was born. Out of crisis. And *the* question that drove these ancient writers and editors was the wisdom question we have been looking at all along: "What is God up to *today, right here and now?*"

Which brings us to the well-known children's story, which is anything but.

Don't Put God in a Box, Unless You Want to Be Swallowed by a Fish

The book of Jonah tells the famous story of the prophet Jonah who wanted nothing to do with his divinely given assignment—to go to the city of Nineveh and *cry out* against it for its *wickedness* (1:2), which is to say, give the city a chance to repent. Nineveh, by the way, was the capital of Assyria, which sacked the northern kingdom, Israel, in 722 BCE and continued to harass the southern kingdom, Judah, throughout the seventh century BCE until the Babylonians gained control of the region.

The Assyrian army was relentless and nearly invincible and (judging from Assyrian artwork) impaled and skinned those who resisted.* I don't want to use an inappropriate analogy, but God's willingness to give the Ninevites a chance to repent while they were at the height of their destructive power might be compared to giving Stalin a chance to repent while he was starving millions of Russian farmers or Hitler while he was slaughtering millions of Jews. Who—with any active sense of justice—would want to give them a chance to repent of their wicked ways?! They need to be judged and sentenced. Why in heaven's name would God show any compassion to our enemies who mean to destroy us?

So, Jonah wanted nothing to do with these godless warmongering bullies for fear they might actually listen and repent. To escape God, Jonah boarded a ship heading the exact opposite direction, but when storms threatened to sink the vessel, Jonah confessed to the crew that he was responsible for unleashing God's wrath on them; if they simply tossed him overboard, they would survive, which they did only too eagerly. And this is where a large fish swallows Jonah, which for some reason is thought to make for a great children's story, though that isn't at all what we're interested in here.

This little incident caused Jonah to reconsider his decision, so when the fish vomited him up onto the shore, he headed to Nineveh—but still copping an attitude. He begrudgingly delivered the shortest and

---

* I'm not kidding. Google "Lachish reliefs" and check out how the Assyrians depicted their sack of Lachish (just southwest of Jerusalem) in 701 BCE.

most negative sales pitch ever, *Forty days more, and Nineveh shall be overthrown* (3:4), and then stomped away. Despite his efforts to subvert God's will, Jonah's worst fears were realized: the people and the king repented, and so *God changed his mind about the calamity that he had said he would bring upon them; and he did not do it* (3:10). Ugh. Could this day get any worse?

That's a great story and echoes the words of Jesus: *Love your enemies and pray for those who persecute you*, for in doing so you will be *perfect . . . as your heavenly Father is perfect* (Matt. 5:44, 48).

The book of another prophet, Nahum, however, tells another story about what God thinks of the Ninevites: he hates them. Nahum in fact celebrates the demise of Nineveh and interprets it as an act of God. The book concludes: *There is no assuaging your hurt, your wound is mortal. All who hear the news about you clap their hands over you. For who has ever escaped your endless cruelty?* (3:19). Translation: God destroyed Nineveh and everyone cheers as if it were the golden goal in the World Cup finals.

Jonah and Nahum clearly see the matter of God's attitude toward the Ninevites differently, and the reason is . . . wait for it . . . *they were written at different times and under different circumstances for different purposes.*

Nahum lived at the time of the fall of Nineveh and, historically speaking, he was right. Nineveh fell to the Babylonians in 612 BCE and, as all prophets do, Nahum interpreted the event as an act of God. Jonah, however, was written in the postexilic period, after (perhaps generations after) the return from Babylonian exile in 538 BCE. And this author doesn't seem to be in the least bit interested in recording history.

The author knew as well as everyone else that Nineveh and the Assyrian Empire had actually fallen. Had the Assyrians actually repented, it would have amounted to a mass shift in religious commitment and political strategy, which would have been big news ("Assyrians bow the knee to Israel's God. Hostilities cease. Film at 11:00"). But nothing of the sort is known from any ancient record, Assyrian or otherwise. It strains credulity.

And then there's the whole "Jonah swallowed by a fish" part of the story. Jonah remains there for three days as the fish descends down, down, even entering the abode of the dead, which the Bible calls Sheol. These strike me as the kinds of details a writer, including an ancient one, would put into a story to ensure that his readers knew they were dealing with something other than history. The book of Jonah isn't a history lesson. It's a parable to challenge its readers to *reimagine* a God bigger than the one they were familiar with.

One of my biggest life lessons about God came when I left home for a "foreign country," namely, graduate school. While working on my PhD, I got to know a lot of people—students and professors— who had religious outlooks very different from mine. It sobered me to see how differently they conceived of God, if at all, and that they were products of their worlds as much as I was a product of mine. And so rather than think of them as pitiful outsiders to God's great plan, I began to do some serious soul searching about whether God might be more merciful and more inclusive than I had always been taught.

The writer of Jonah, living sometime after the exile, had a similar experience and wrote to a community that would have understood his point. While in Babylonian captivity, the Judahites no doubt got to know their hosts quite well. They raised children and buried relatives there. Familiarity breeds acceptance, and when the Persians gave the all-clear for the Judahites to return home, many actually decided to stay behind. In fact, Babylon would become a center of Jewish life and thought for the next thousand years. (The Babylonian Talmud, the authoritative book of Judaism, was produced there.)

And so the writer of Jonah told a story of God's expansive mercy for non-Israelites; in other words, maybe God cares for other people too. And the author used as his illustration a clearly fictionalized account of their long-gone ancient foe to express his newfound belief, or at least hope, that God is more inclusive than they were giving God credit for.

Travel broadens, as they say. Coming into contact with different people and cultures cannot help but affect our view of ourselves, the world we live in—and God. Both Nahum and Jonah are works of wisdom, of reimaging God to make sense of current experience in the here and now.

I'd like to think—and in fact I do think—that the portrait of God in Jonah is closer to what God is like: that God does not rejoice in wiping people out, but desires to commune with people of every tribe and nation. But that's just me. Without a moment's hesitation, I will say that I favor one story over the other, because it makes more sense to me, as that sense is informed by other experiences that I and those I know have had of God and especially given what I understand of God in my time and place as a Christian.

But that's just me. The more important point to raise is that the very presence of both Nahum and Jonah in our Bible forces us *all* to ponder what God is like in our here and now *just as these authors did.*

I may be wrong in *how* I process what God is like, of course, but I am not wrong *because* I process what God is like.

Our diverse Bible demands that we employ wisdom when we read it. It keeps reminding us that we too need to accept our sacred responsibility to sense how God is present in our here and now.

Rewriting History

The Bible is relentless in modeling for us wisdom—reading the moment, never detached from the sacred tradition but never simply repeating it, because God is always present and on the move. And so we can never just read the Bible without also pondering it, with creativity and imagination, just like the biblical authors, in order to bring these ancient oracles into our own lives. From the second we pick up the Bible and start reading it, we are drawn into an act that requires wisdom.

We could go on and on with a lot of great examples from the Bible to support the point, but I'd like to give just one more: the books of 1 and 2 Chronicles. You know, those books that nobody ever reads because they basically repeat those boring stories of Israel's kings you just slogged through in 1 and 2 Samuel and 1 and 2 Kings. But stick with me. You might come to love these books, or at least hate them less.

The books of 1 Samuel through 2 Kings tell the five-hundred-year story of Israel's monarchy from the first king, Saul (sometime before 1000 BCE), until the Babylonian exile. In my experience most people who try to read all four books one after the other usually scoop their eyes out with a spoon somewhere in the middle of 1 Kings. To actually finish 2 Kings requires a miracle. Continuing on with 1 and 2 Chronicles is superhuman. And I'm pretty sure Jesus would agree.*

It doesn't help that these latter two books come right after 2 Kings. That's just bad product placement, though that's only the case in Christian Bibles. In the Jewish Bible, these books are found at the very end. Why? Because that's where they belong. But why? Because Chronicles is not a repeat of 1 Samuel through 2 Kings. *It is a retelling of those books from a much later point in Jewish history.* In fact, it is nothing less than an act of reimaging God.

To make a long story short, 1 Samuel through 2 Kings were probably written before and during the Babylonian exile, and the main question these books address is, "How did we get into this mess? What did we do to deserve exile?" The short answer is, "You committed apostasy by worshiping foreign gods, with your kings leading the way." In other words, these books interpret events of history and pronounce a guilty verdict on Judah.

But 1 and 2 Chronicles were written centuries later, probably no earlier than about 400 BCE and more likely closer to 300 or even a bit later—so somewhere in the middle of the Persian period (which began in 538) and perhaps as late as the Greek period (which began with the conquest by the Greeks under Alexander the Great in 332). And these books answer a different question altogether, not "What did we do to deserve this?" but "After all this time, is God still with us?"

---

* While we're on the subject, the books of Samuel, Kings, and Chronicles were not originally written in two parts. They were just really long, so when the original Hebrew was translated into Greek (more on this later), someone figured, "Hey, these are long. Let's make each of them two books." And apparently someone else said, "Okay. That's a great bit of marketing, turning three boring books into six. I don't see the downside." And there you have it.

Once again, we revisit our theme: as times changed, the ancient Jews had to reprocess what it meant to be the chosen people—if indeed that label even meant anything anymore.

Seeing how these late postexilic Jews reprocessed their entire history is for me (and I'm not kidding), *the most exciting part of the Old Testament, because 1 and 2 Chronicles are nothing less than one big act of reimagining God*, of accepting the sacred responsibility to creatively retell the past in order to bridge that past to a difficult present and thus to hear God's voice afresh once again.

And just how creative these books are is evident by how different they are, page after page, from the earlier history in 1 Samuel through 2 Kings. One story—the reign of King Manasseh—gets to the heart of it.

King Manasseh appears in 2 Kings 21:1–18, where he is absolutely the wickedest loser king in the entire Bible. During his long fifty-five-year reign (the longest of any of the Old Testament kings), Manasseh was all kinds of stupid. If there was a way to incite God's anger, he found it—including the unthinkable: he systematically erected centers of pagan worship, including in the Temple itself, sacrificed his own son, and *shed very much innocent blood, until he had filled Jerusalem from one end to another* (2 Kings 21:16).

Manasseh was so wicked that the author credits him entirely for the destruction of Jerusalem by the Babylonians a few generations later. Even the sweeping reforms and deep devotion to the Law of his grandson Josiah—who is praised by the writer as no other—weren't enough to cancel out Manasseh's wickedness: *Still the LORD did not turn from the fierceness of his great wrath, by which his anger was kindled against Judah, because of all the provocations with which Manasseh had provoked him* (2 Kings 23:26).

The story of Manasseh in 2 Chronicles 33 also starts out with a hefty list of Manasseh's sins, but that's where the similarities end and creative differences begin. According to this author, Manasseh's sins did not lead to Judah's exile—but to *his* exile: the Assyrian army took *Manasseh* captive to *Babylon*. This incident is not mentioned in 2 Kings—because it didn't happen. There was no Assyrian invasion to remove one Judahite king, and if there were, they wouldn't have taken him to Babylon!

At this point the author is screaming at us to see his account of Manasseh, like the story of Jonah, as something other than "straight history."

We read next that Manasseh, while in Babylonian captivity, humbled himself and repented of his considerable list of sins. So God returned him from Babylon and *restored him again to Jerusalem and to his kingdom*, where he continued to live out his remaining years as a righteous king, a repentant and restored Manasseh (33:10–17). Not exactly in harmony with 2 Kings.

So what caused the national exile according to 2 Chronicles if not Manasseh's sins? The people were at fault. They followed the repentant Manasseh in restricting their worship to Yahweh alone, yet they continued to worship Yahweh by sacrificing at the *high places*, altars erected here and there, rather than in the Temple alone. This author couldn't ignore the exile, but he did give it a different cause. The people were to blame, not Manasseh.

The reign of King Manasseh in 2 Chronicles—with his deportation to Babylon, repentance, and return to his homeland—is not an account of Manasseh's reign. It is a *symbolic retelling of Judah's exile and return home after the captives had learned their lesson and repented of their sins*.

This retelling of the reign of Manasseh is like a sermon illustration for one of the central themes of 1 and 2 Chronicles, which we've also seen in Ezekiel 18 (he of the sour grapes): God treats you as *you* deserve. As 2 Chronicles 7:14 puts it: *If my people who are called by my name humble themselves, pray, seek my face, and turn from their wicked ways, then I will hear from heaven, and will forgive their sin and heal their land.* That is also how Manasseh is described in 2 Chronicles.

Life was probably somewhat discouraging for this author and his audience. It's good to be back in the promised land, but centuries had passed since Judah last had a king on the throne. When will God restore them to their former glory?! When will they once again experience God's favor and blessing?! Those were the active questions of their day. Not, "What did we do to get into this mess?" as the author of 1 and 2 Kings was asking, but, "How much longer do we have to wait for a sign that God hasn't abandoned us?"

The story of Manasseh, the penitent sinner restored to the place of God's favor, is a reminder to that audience that God will fully heal them too—if they humble themselves and repent. After all, if even Manasseh back then could repent and be forgiven, surely God will do the same for you here and now if you repent. That is the moral of the story, and to tell that story the author reshaped the past—intentionally, transparently, undeniably—to let the past speak to a very new and different situation.*

That is to say, the retelling of the reign of Manasseh (and 1 and 2 Chronicles as a whole) is an act of wisdom—of reading the moment

---

* This story continued to resonate with Jews of later generations. Centuries after Chronicles was written, an unknown Jew imagined what Manasseh's prayer of repentance might have looked like, giving us a short book known as the Prayer of Manasseh, which can be found in the Apocrypha.

and reimagining what God is doing and, more important, what God will do in the (hopefully not too distant) future.

* * *

Rethinking the past in view of changing times is about much more than simply rethinking the past. It is that, of course, but it is also about a much grander matter that I hope hasn't been buried too deeply in the many details we've been looking at.

What was ultimately at stake for the ancient writers wasn't simply how they perceived the past, but how they perceived God now.

That's why they couldn't simply leave the past in the past, but transposed it to their present. They did so not because these ancient stories in and of themselves held power, but because of what these ancient stories said about God. They were the means by which the people connected with the God of old and brought this God into the present. And what drove them to forge this link with God was the crisis of the moment, whether the fall of the north in 722 BCE, the fall of the south in 586 BCE, or being ruled by a succession of foreigners in the centuries thereafter—Persians, then Greeks, then Romans.

Seeing the Bible as a book of wisdom, which doesn't hand us answers but invites us to accept our journey of faith with courage and humility, is a new idea, I suspect, for some reading this book. And that's why I've tried to give some examples and go into some detail, so we can see for ourselves how the Bible actually works—even though, truth be told, we are just scratching the surface.

I hope too that another vital point—perhaps *the* point—I am trying to make hasn't been too obscured by talking on and on about Assyrians, slave laws, and eating sour grapes. Watching how the Bible behaves as a book of wisdom rather than a set-in-stone rulebook is more than just a textual curiosity to be noted and set aside. Rather, it models for us the normalcy of seeking the presence of God for ourselves in our here and now.

Like that of the biblical writers themselves, our sacred responsibility is to engage faithfully and seriously enough the stories of the past in order to faithfully and seriously reimagine God in our present moment. The Bible doesn't end that process of reimagination. It promotes it.

Isn't this what all this Jesus business is about, anyway, asking anew, "What is God like?" We're getting there. But first, the universe.

Chapter 6

What Is God Like?

The Universe Freaks Me Out

At some point I stopped thinking of God as "up there somewhere." I'm not sure exactly when, but I do know why: I was born in the twentieth century.

I went to school along with everybody else and (when I was paying attention) learned about galaxies, solar systems, red shifts, and the Crab Nebula. I learned that, technically speaking, there is no "up there" to begin with. That idea only works with a flat earth, not a round one. I also learned that, technically speaking, the universe has no "center"—no point is any more or less central than any other. I'm still quite dense about how that's even possible, but I've entrusted the matter to the kinds of people who never got picked for dodgeball in junior high school.

I find it a bit unsettling, though, that had I been born in a Viking fishing village or medieval Anglo-Saxon farm, none of this would have come to mind, and I could have gone on with my sorry, laborious life praying to the gods for a good harvest. But, as it turns out, I had no real control about when and where I was born. It just happened, and had I been born at another place in time, it wouldn't have actually been me anyway (if you follow me).

And so I have lived my entire life in an age of unparalleled scientific advancements, and the fact of my existence here and now, not then and there, certainly influences how I think about everything, including what or who God is.

I cannot keep my existence at bay when I think about God. I can't step outside of my humanity and see things from above. The biblical writers didn't even do that, so please don't ask me to try. Maybe we're not even meant to. But now we're jumping ahead of ourselves.

Back to the universe.

I wanted to be an astronomer when I was young, until I found out you need math. But I still think a lot about what's out there—though not in a dreamy, contemplative, healthy, awed kind of way, but in a the-longer-I-think-about-it-the-worse-I-feel sort of way.

King David wrote a really nice psalm about three thousand years ago praising God for how wonderful the heavens are (Ps. 19), which is fine for him, but he had it easy. His "universe" consisted of a flat earth of manageable size, with a dome overhead where the sun, moon, and stars hung out. Above the dome was water (hence the blue sky) and above that somewhere was the heavenly realm where God was seated on his throne. And all of this was, from David's point of view, probably a couple of thousand years old or so, which I'm sure felt like a long time to him.

With all due respect to Israel's primo king, David and I are not on the same page here. I'm more with the seventeenth-century philosopher Blaise Pascal, who lived when modern science was coming into its own, and who had public nervous breakdowns in his *Pensées* such as: "The eternal silence of these infinite spaces terrifies me."

Hardly the stuff of King David's praises. Given the vastness of space, which was only beginning to be discovered at his time, Pascal questioned the meaning and purpose of his own comparatively puny little life on one puny little planet at one puny little point in time.* A man after my own heart. If he were alive today, I'd introduce him to light speed, black holes, the multiverse, the red shift, and string theory just to see if I can make a Frenchman spontaneously combust.

The *known* universe (apparently there's even more to it) is about 13.8 billion years old. If we compressed those years into a single calendar year, with the big bang at the stroke of midnight on January 1, our galaxy would have been formed on March 16, our solar system on September 2, and the first multicellular life on December 5.

It's almost Christmas, and we're nowhere close to hairless bipeds. I feel we're running out of time.

We'll get to us soon enough, but first the dinosaurs have to arrive, which they do on Christmas Day. Primitive humans with stone tools don't arrive until 10:24 p.m. on New Year's Eve. The Israelites pop up at about 11:59:53 (tick-tock, seven seconds left), Jesus a swift two seconds later, and the last 437 years of our planet's history occur within the last second of the year. My projected life span would take up a little more than one tenth of a second.

And now I'm getting depressed. Why do I do this to myself?

The size of the universe is equally unsettling, and the numbers used to describe it are for all practical purposes meaningless. Traveling at the speed of light (186,282 miles per second), it would take 93 billion years to cross the 546 sextillion miles of the known universe from one end to the other—that's 546 followed by twenty-one zeros.

---

* Blaise Pascal, "Of the Necessity of the Wager," sec. 3, nos. 205–6, in *Pascal's Pensées* (New York: Dutton, 1958), 48.

By the way, did you know that counting up to one billion, one count each second, would take 31.69 years—the age that males finally stop playing beer pong? To count up to 93 billion would take 2,947.17 years. If King David had begun counting as a child, he'd be getting done about now.

Anyway, we don't need to get into all that. My point is simply, no, King David, the heavens are not telling *the glory of God* (Ps. 19:1)—at least not without a lot of heavy theological lifting and perhaps a double bourbon. The heavens actually freak me out and make me wonder whether there is a God at all—at least the God I read about in the Bible, who is said to quaintly fashion everything, like a potter at a wheel.

Yes, let's bring the Bible into this. That's the point of this book, after all.

The God of the Bible

The Bible is, if anything, a book the purpose of which is to tell us what God is like. Some say that "revealing" God to us is the Bible's true purpose. So when the Bible says something about God, people of faith tend to take it to heart, which we do with some enthusiasm when we read that God is the defender of the poor and oppressed, savior of the widow and orphan, champion of the downtrodden, just king and impartial judge of all, shepherd of sheep, rock of security, flowing stream of refreshment, comforter of the sick, and above all (for Christians) the one who sent us Jesus.

I am drawn to this God, believe in this God, though with good and bad days, as have many people of faith for a very long time.

But, to be honest, I—like Pascal—have a lot of trouble squaring this attentive, supportive, and available God with a God who is responsible for this ridiculously large, impersonal, cold, dark, largely empty, frightening, and not at all comforting or inviting universe we live in.

Don't get me wrong, I have nothing against the universe. I *like* the universe, and I'd hate to leave it. But from a faith perspective I'm not sure what it means to say the sorts of things that Christians say about God without a second thought, like God is "up there looking down" and cares for each and every one of us personally—or as Jesus put it, *Even the hairs of your head are all counted* (Matt. 10:30).

Connecting with the God of the Bible would be a lot easier if we didn't know as much—which would be pretty much any time other than this stupid time in world history that all of us were dropped into. Take me back to the carefree days of medieval Europe, with its small, flat, young earth and a dome overhead rather than an infinite universe and infinite time.

It's just a lot to take in is all I'm saying.

And as if science weren't enough to process, believing in the "God of the Bible" is challenging for another reason—at least it is for most people I've encountered.

God seems uncomfortably touchy. It doesn't take much to set him off to kill, plague, or otherwise physically punish these frail human vessels God has created. Swift physical retribution seems to be this God's go-to means of conflict resolution.

We only need to get to the sixth chapter of the Bible to see God already so fed up that he drowns *all flesh in which is the breath of life*— humans *together with animals* (for good measure, I suppose)—except for Noah and his family (eight in all) and two of each kind of animal that God will need for pressing reset and repopulating the earth, plus more animals so the proper appeasing sacrifices can be made, which, given the circumstances, seems like an excellent idea.

Even if we think (as I do) that God didn't actually drown all life on earth except eight humans and a boat full of animals, and that the story of Noah isn't historical, but one of many ancient stories from greater Mesopotamia to explain (it seems) a cataclysmic local (not global) deluge of some sort, that doesn't get us off the hook entirely. We still have the problem that the God of the Bible is portrayed as doing something rather brutal in the first place and so early in the game.

Was that the only solution? Was there no backup plan? Was this the only conceivable way forward?

Is this what the God of the 546-sextillion-mile-in-diameter universe is really like? Is the God of all there is, was, and ever will be also so quick to erase humanity off this speck of dust we call home like someone hosing grass clippings off the driveway? That just seems out of character to me for a God who set in motion the galaxies, with all their mystery, awe, and incomprehensibility. Is a God like that really going to melt down in Genesis 6 like a frazzled ill-equipped parent of a toddler?

And this same God will later, with disturbing regularity, rain down plagues, pestilence, and war on his own people, the Israelites, when they disobey, not to mention command the annihilation of Israel's enemies and hand out death sentences to adulterers, perjurers, young men who dishonor their parents, and those who falsely claim that a woman is a virgin.

The Bible says a lot about God that is comforting, encouraging, and inspiring, but at other times not so much. The Bible sends us conflicting messages about what this God is like. *The LORD is my shepherd* or *Even though I walk through the darkest valley* (Ps. 23:1, 4) aren't always enough to balance out *I am going to . . . destroy . . . all flesh in which is the breath of life* (Gen. 6:17) or *Take the blasphemer outside the camp . . . and stone him* (Lev. 24:14).

Making sense of this God creates challenges for me, and when I bring the universe into it, I don't mind saying once again, I have a hard time connecting the God of back there and then with my world here and now.

And I'm not the only one. I know many people *of faith* who struggle regularly with the God of the Bible, because this God seems so locked in a world we don't recognize, a world that is so distant from ours—a world we have worked hard to get over. I know others who say this God isn't worth the trouble and therefore choose to believe in no God at all.

No one should underestimate the force of this dilemma or the stress and pain it creates for people trying to believe. Those who have a hard time with the God of the Bible can't be dismissed as faithless rebels against God's word. Some want to have faith—but they also want to have integrity. They live here and now, not there and then, yet they have this ancient Bible and a Christian faith bound fast to it, and the way forward feels like walking on a razor's edge between two options—belief in the absurd God or belief that the idea of God is absurd.

The Wisdom Question for All of Us

So what do we do about this? We could try not thinking about it. If that works for some, I don't feel it's my place to interfere, but it doesn't help me or others I know. If faith in God means having to keep the universe and the Bible under an invisibility cloak, that's much more stressful for me than trying to work it through. What kind of God would give us minds with which to ponder our existence and then expect us to clamp down the lid when we actually ponder?

I just don't think that we are meant to isolate ourselves from our time and place as we think about God—in fact, *we can't.* And with that we are getting to the point of all this.

We are who we are and when we are, and rather than avoid these facts of life, we should look this challenge square in the face and (stop me if you've heard this already) *embrace the sacred responsibility* of asking a question that I feel is at least as important as any other we can ask, if not more so: *What is God like?*

That question isn't just for children in Sunday school, so they learn to check off the right box. It's a wisdom question.

In fact, "What is God like?" is *the* wisdom question around which all others revolve, the question that is ever before us, as each successive generation tries to pass on the faith of the past, which comes to us from an ancient time and in an ancient book, to the next generation that occupies its own unique moment in time and space.

Having faith in God does not mean having to keep our distance from our own humanity. We should be fully connected to it and honest about what we are thinking—though we also must operate with humility and trust in this infinite Creator of infinite spaces. That paradox is the true perspective of faith—not fear that makes us retreat from our humanity, but faith that encourages us as humans to explore it in God's uncontrolled presence.

And so, as a person of faith who studies the Bible for a living and who also lives (as I mentioned) in the here and now, I have come to terms somewhat with this dilemma of matching the God of the Bible with my faith: *The God I read about in the Bible is not what God is like—in some timeless abstraction, and that's that—but how God was imagined and then reimagined by ancient people of faith living in real times and places.*

By "imagined" I don't mean the biblical writers made up God out of thin air. I believe these ancient people experienced the Divine. But *how they experienced* God and therefore *how they thought and wrote* about God were filtered through their experience, when and where they existed.

At least I hope so, because it would certainly explain an awful lot.

And to give a preview of where I'm going with all this, not only in this chapter but in the ones to follow, *reimagining God for one's here and now is what Christians and Jews have been doing ever since there have been Christians and Jews, and invariably so, because we are people.* And that process of reimagination began, as we've already seen, within the pages of the Bible itself.

The sacred responsibility I've been talking about is really a call to follow this biblical lead by reimagining God in our time and place.

There. That pretty much sums up the entire book. I hope you have your highlighter handy.

As full-fledged card-carrying humans, we don't have a choice. We are all culturally embedded creatures—we can never untangle ourselves from our here and now. We perceive God, think about God, and talk about God in ways that make sense to us by virtue of when and where we live.

Imagining a boundless God from within our bounded moment in time is a paradox of faith—*as inescapable for us as it was for the biblical writers.* And when we reimagine God for ourselves and do so deliberately, consciously, and as an act of faith, we find ourselves, once again, walking the path of wisdom—in principle no different from wondering how or whether to answer a fool, what it means to remember the sabbath, how to treat slaves, or rewriting the story of King Manasseh. *We reimagine God in ways that account for and make sense of our experience.*

Lying just below the surface of all the things we've peeked at to this point is this God question. It's not really about fools, sabbath keeping, or which slaves get to go free, but "What does it mean for God to be present here and now, in this moment in which I find myself? What does God's presence look like right now, and how is that like and unlike God's presence in those other human moments in generations past?"

Whether we are aware of it or not, behind our religious deliberations, in one form or another, we are really asking a deeply foundational question, "What kind of God do I believe in, really?" This is not a luxury question for those with idle time on their hands, but exactly the kind of question we should deliberately bring to the front of our consciousness as an *expression of responsible faith*; it is not evidence that our faith is weakening.

And, once again, the Bible—simply by being its ancient, ambiguous, and diverse self—invites us to engage this God question for ourselves. Even here, where the topic is the very nature of God, the Bible simply doesn't let us sit back as spectators, but summons us on a journey of wisdom along with the biblical writers themselves who trod this same path long before.

We're Stuck Being Human

Where do we see the biblical writers imagining God within the boundaries of their time and place? Simply put, everywhere. There is no God-talk in the Bible that isn't already filtered through human experience.

The ancient languages the Bible was written in—Hebrew, Greek, and a little Aramaic—are not some special divine code dropped down from heaven. The languages of the Bible were quite ordinary—more like what you'd find in a TV ad than in the polished work of a poet laureate. These languages developed ("evolved" is really the better word) in a particular part of the world over time and were spoken by ordinary people from peasant to king. And those ordinary languages were then called upon to do the extraordinary: speak about the boundless Creator.

So even on that most basic level of language, God is known through our human experience. In fact, the Creator *must* condescend to our humanity in order to be understood—as any parent will remind us. Parents have to stoop down to their children's level to speak into their world. Expecting children to operate at their parents' level is bad parenting.

Or grandparenting. As I write this, my granddaughter is eleven months old, and I say things to her like, "How big is Lilah? Hoooow big iiiis Lilah?! She's soooooooooooo big." And of course she laughs and throws her little arms up in the air. I have to talk to her like that, because if I tried, "Lilah, let me tell you about this book I'm writing about reimagining God," she might just reach for my nose.

Those ancient languages were used to describe God in ways that made sense to the ancient writers—so Yahweh is a shepherd, a king, a warrior, a gardener, and so forth. Those descriptions of God were taken from the surrounding world. God isn't actually a shepherd, but God cares for Israel the way a shepherd cares for his flock. God isn't actually a king, but God is *like* a king.

In a way, when the biblical writers look at God, they all reflect back something of their own experience as humans living in a particular time in a particular culture. They use familiar metaphors when speaking of God. They don't—"poof"—magically take off their cultural lenses.

No one does.

To do so would be to cease being human, which I don't believe God is asking any of us to do.

As I said earlier, I don't mean to say that the biblical writers were simply *creating* God out of their experience from the ground up. But still, the only means they had at their disposal for *talking about* God were the language and the thoughts of that point in the human drama that they happened to occupy.

And that holds not only for the tenth century BCE, but also for us in the twenty-first century CE who have learned how big the universe is.

God alone is God, so the words and thoughts we use can never be equated with God; when we make that false equation, we are actually limiting God. Although—and I think this is just as important to emphasize—human words and thoughts are also *adequate* for talking about God within each cultural moment. And no human culture is *more* equipped to speak of God than any other—and that most certainly includes my own Western, white, male tradition that has tended to think of itself as the norm for everyone else.

Yes, what we think God is like and how any of us talk about God may not be the final word, but they are still adequate. Maybe that is how all our God-talk is. Maybe (if I may venture beyond my horizon) that is precisely how God intended us to think and talk about God, as people in our time and place, because God is fine with our being human. After all, this God, as Christians claim, walked among us.

Wisdom teaches us to embrace both the adequacy *and* the limitations of our God-talk, to keep the two in tension. Perhaps accepting that paradox is true faith. And the Bible—in all its ancient, ambiguous, diverse weirdness—models for us how invariably limited any God-talk is, to make sure that we don't ever come to think that we have reached the end of the rainbow.

Psalm 68—to take a quick example—says that God *rides upon the clouds* (verse 4), an image also used to describe the ancient Canaanite storm god Baal. I don't mind saying that I don't think God rides a chariot across the sky to make weather or for any other reason—but the *ancient* Israelites certainly seemed to. Or at least they found the metaphor helpful. But I don't.

And I think it's perfectly fine to say with firm conviction that we don't think like that anymore, because we see the heavens differently and therefore God differently. This doesn't make the ancient Israelites "wrong" or "unsophisticated." It makes them human. Neither should it make us snobs who think we "get it" more than others. We, too, are human, seeing God from the limitations of our own time and place in ways we probably don't even realize.

And what if God is just fine with our being human?

Recognizing how our thinking of God is bound to our own time and place is freeing in that it helps us make sense of some of the rather uncomfortable things we read about God in the Bible, like Psalm 68—or the following that has caused more than its share of quiet panic among alert Bible readers.

The Israelites believed something about God that would get some of us in very hot water today if we uttered the thought in polite

Christian company. As we saw earlier, just like every other ancient people of biblical times, the Israelites believed that *many gods existed* and that their God (Yahweh) *was one of them.*

Not "the only God," but one of the gods.

And just like their ancient neighbors with their own religions, the Israelites believed that their national god was the highest and best among all the gods. But as Moses's warning illustrates, these other gods nevertheless had a purpose.

> *And when you look up to the heavens and see the sun, the moon, and the stars, all the host of heaven, do not be led astray and bow down to them and serve them,* **things that the LORD your God has allotted to all the peoples everywhere under heaven.** *But the LORD has taken you and brought you out of the iron-smelter, out of Egypt, to become* **a people of his very own possession,** *as you are now.* (Deut. 4:19–20)

Translation: "Worshiping the sun, moon, and stars is what I set up for all the other nations. But you, Israel, are mine. You worship me only." At least here, it seems as though God really doesn't have a problem with other religions for other people.

What made the Israelites different from their neighbors, religiously speaking, was their belief that *only* Yahweh, and *not any of the other gods* (heavenly bodies included), was worthy of their worship. To use the technical language, the Israelites were not monotheists in the strict sense of the word, but monolatrists: they *worshiped* one God, but *believed in the existence* of many gods.*

---

* Monolatry comes from the Greek *mono*, "one," and *latreia*, "worship."

All of which is to say, when it came to worshiping something, the ancient Israelites had options. I don't mean in some poetic way, as when preachers today speak about the "false god" of money or politics. The Israelites of long ago believed that other gods really, actually existed and that these real, actual gods could do real, actual things to them—like withhold rain, give victory to the enemy, or send a plague of locusts.

I can understand how odd this "one God among many gods" idea may sound, but it's the Bible itself that drove the idea home for me— one story in particular, truly one of the stranger and more unnerving passages in all of the Old Testament, a story that might get a lot more attention, were it not buried in the middle of a rather long and tedious section of the Old Testament that recounts the five-hundred-year line of Israel's kings.

Looking at that story and others like it may put us in a weird place for a few moments, but it will drive home a central point about how the Bible works.

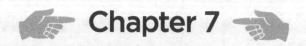

Chapter 7

Imagining and Reimagining God

You Mean to Tell Me That Actually Worked?

Around the year 850 BCE, almost one hundred years after Israel split into the northern and southern kingdoms, King Mesha of Moab rebelled against the north. Moab was one of Israel's eastern neighbors, on the other side of the Jordan River, and had been under the thumb of the north for about a century. The northern king, Jehoram, understandably couldn't let this go, so he mustered his troops and, along with the help of the king of the southern kingdom, Jehoshaphat (as in "jumpin' Jehoshaphat"), and an unnamed king of nearby Edom, went to put Mesha in his place.

The story, told in 2 Kings 3, may sound as interesting as watching plaque form on your teeth, and for the most part it is—until we get to the end of the story. The outnumbered Moabites were pinned inside a walled city. Out of conventional options, Mesha did what any of us would have done in his position: he sacrificed to his god his firstborn son on the city wall.

Ha. Just kidding. We'd never do that. But, wow, what a zany pagan king that Mesha was, thinking that sacrificing his son and successor to his fictional god (Chemosh) would actually do any good!! Can you believe these people? Well, thank goodness the Bible will set him right. There are no other gods, child sacrifice is barbaric, and—obviously—this won't work.

Except it does.

After Mesha sacrifices his son, we read: *And great wrath came upon Israel, so they [the Israelite-led coalition] withdrew from him [Mesha] and returned to their own land* (2 Kings 3:27).*

And that's how this story ends. No explanation. As if this is just what happens now and then when an enemy king sacrifices his son to a god. The biblical writers really should have thought ahead and included "footnotes for modern Christians."

Banking Options

Here might be yet another ideal place to remind ourselves that these stories were written a very long time ago: Mesha's rebellion is about as far back in time for us as about the year 4900 CE is forward in time.

That distance always stops me dead in my tracks. We're talking about a long time ago, in the Iron Age, which archaeologists date to 1200–500 BCE and is so called because ancient people figured out that iron made better weapons than bronze. People thought differently back then about a lot of things, not least of which was an assumed and universal belief in a very active divine realm where all sorts of gods went about their business. The responsibility of mere

---

* Archaeologists actually found a Moabite account of Mesha's rebellion carved into a three-foot-tall standing stone monument referred to by archaeologists (always known for their flare for the creative) as the Moabite Stone. It differs in focus and details from the biblical version, as one would expect, but ends in generally the same way: thanks to his god, Chemosh, Mesha won.

mortals was to make sure these gods thought well of them, so mortals could do things like grow crops, have a water supply, produce children, and wage war successfully—in other words, not die.

But gods are fickle beings. Your comfort is not high on their priority list, and they can turn on you for reasons that would keep mortals guessing. One thing is for sure, however. When things were going badly for a nation, that meant one or more of its gods was clearly displeased and needed to be appeased by an offering, normally slitting an animal's throat and burning it on a stone altar. In cases of extreme need, such as the one in which we find our King Mesha, you pull out all the stops and sacrifice your beloved child.

Mesha's move, though hardly easy for him, made sense in his world. He appeased his high god, Chemosh, with a sacrifice the deity couldn't refuse. With divine pleasure restored, a _wrath_ fell upon the Israelite-led coalition, and they were repelled.

And all of this leads me to my point for bringing up the wild and wacky world of Iron Age religion. _The biblical storyteller not only is clearly on board with the idea that Mesha's sacrifice worked, but didn't even feel the need to explain the concept to his readers._

Neither does the writer explain why Yahweh didn't interfere at that point and give the Israelites a glorious victory despite the sacrifice. I mean, I would expect to read, "And yet, Chemosh was still powerless to stop Israel's Yahweh-backed victory." Perhaps Yahweh didn't want to back a coalition led by the northern kingdom (the writers of 1 and 2 Kings have nothing good to say about the north). We don't know, but what we do know is that the writer accepted without explanation or hesitation the notion that other gods actually exist, can be appeased, and have the power to affect the course of human affairs. It's just a given.

Yes, Virginia, other gods do exist—at least the Israelites thought so, along with all their ancient neighbors. That notion takes some getting used to for us, but it might (or might not) help to remember that the ancient biblical writer really had no choice about what to make of Mesha's last-minute rescue.

The writer was part of a world that imagined the divine realm this way, and he can hardly be faulted. Any of us would have done the same.

Today we don't have a heavenly realm full of gods, but we do have a lot of banks, which means we have loads of banking options. Banks vie for our business by comparing themselves to other banks—"We are more friendly, have more locations, better interest rates, free checking," and so forth. All competing banks claim, "We are the place to trust with your financial lives, not those dozens of other options you pass on the street day after day."

And now we know how ancient religions work.

For Iron Age humans, the thought that all those higher powers vying for human devotion didn't actually exist would have been as nonsensical as it would be for someone to tell us, "Oh, those other banks aren't *real*. And those other ATMs don't actually spit out money. They are empty. There *are* no other banking options."

The active question for us is not, "Which is the only bank that truly exists?" but "Where do you bank?" Likewise, Iron Age peoples asked, "Which god (or gods) are you devoted to? Which do you pray to and sacrifice to? Which do you worship?"

It would be bizarre indeed to think that the Israelites somehow kept a safe distance from this ancient understanding of the gods—and stories like Mesha's sacrifice tell us they didn't.

The Israelites certainly believed other gods existed, but Yahweh alone was to be worshiped because he was the *best* god. How they thought and wrote about their God was absolutely shaped by the world in which they lived—which is a very different world from ours.

And this brings us to one of the best-known stories in the Bible, which is also the closest the Bible comes to a pay-per-view UFC cage match: the exodus from Egypt.

What Does God Have to Be Jealous About?

The exodus story is one of the better known in the entire Bible: Moses leads the Hebrew slaves out of Egypt after Pharaoh and the Egyptians suffer through ten plagues.

These plagues aren't random displays of Yahweh's might, but a dramatic face-off between the story's two central characters. In this corner we have Yahweh, the God of Israel, local god, god over slaves, newcomer on the world stage, making grandiose claims yet largely untested, and represented by his servant Moses. And in the other corner we have the reigning and undisputed perennial world champions, the tag team of Egyptian gods represented by the priests and above all by their Pharaoh.

At stake was whether Yahweh or Pharaoh would claim Israel as his own. And in case you somehow missed *The Ten Commandments* on TV for the past sixty years, Yahweh wins. Easily. Like, no contest.

Yahweh's opening move in the first plague is to turn the Nile to blood. Impressive, yes, but also brimming with religious significance. The Nile was *the* reason Egypt existed at all—its yearly flooding of the banks allowed for life in an otherwise barren land. The Nile deity Hapi was to be thanked personally and profusely for making this happen like clockwork, thus keeping the Egyptians from dying. Yahweh's first plague shows his superiority over a key Egyptian deity.

In the second plague, Yahweh multiplies frogs all over Egypt. Okay. Whatever. Why not something more threatening, like puppies? Why frogs? Because the Egyptian goddess of fertility and childbirth, Heqet, is depicted with the head of a (wait for it) frog. An out-of-control mass of frogs was a religious statement: Heqet is unable to do her job of governing fertility when confronted by the more powerful Yahweh.

If you want to be an awesome god in Egypt or anywhere in the ancient world, you definitely want to control water and fertility, the forces of life. The first two plagues depict a God of slaves marching into Egyptian territory and smacking around two of their vital deities.

To mention just two more, in the ninth plague (darkness), Yahweh neuters the sun god Ra, the high Egyptian god and Pharaoh's patron god, by blotting out the sun for three days. Then in the tenth plague, Yahweh brings death to the firstborn of Egypt, thus pinning to the mat the god of death, Osiris (or Anubis). The whole cosmic battle is summed up nicely in Exodus 12:12, where Yahweh tells Moses, *On all the gods of Egypt I will execute judgments*. You can say that again, Yahweh. You can say that again. Yahweh frees the Israelite slaves by beating the Egyptian gods into submission.

For this story to have any punch (pun intended), we need to see that, to the ancient Israelites, the gods of Egypt were actually real and Yahweh actually did kick their actual (figurative) butts. *We* might not think that Egyptian gods ever existed (mark me down for that), but how *we* imagine God is 110 percent irrelevant at the moment. How *we* see things is exactly what we need to get over if we want to understand stories like this one. The Israelites *did* believe Yahweh conquered the Egyptian gods—and if we bury that lede, we miss the point of this ancient story.

Israel's "founding narrative"—the departure from Egypt and ascent to nationhood—is an odd and ancient story of rumbling deities where Yahweh easily comes out on top.

The lesson continues. About three months after they left Egypt, the former slaves arrive at their destination, the mountain of God, Mt. Sinai, to meet their hero-warrior God and await further instruction. Yahweh soon summons Moses to hike up the mountain to receive the Ten Commandments, and the *first thing out of Yahweh's mouth* is:

> *I am Yahweh* your God, who brought you out of the land of Egypt, out of the house of slavery;* **you shall have no other gods before me**. (Exod. 20:2–3)

This is the first of the Ten Commandments, and it's good and proper to start with the most important one, which reiterates what just happened in Egypt. But having no other gods *before* Yahweh

---

* As mentioned earlier, English translations replace the divine name "Yahweh" with "LORD" out of respect for Jewish tradition. The reason I prefer to use the divine name here and there is only to remind us of the point of this chapter, that the Israelites had a God with a proper name just as all the other nations had gods with their own names: Baal of the Canaanites, Chemosh of the Moabites, Milcom of the Ammonites, and so forth.

(meaning "in preference to" Yahweh) is a command that only has force if real live divine options are available.

The command does not say, "Remember that there are no other gods out there," but, "Don't even think about sharing your allegiance with any of them." After all, Yahweh *alone* delivered the Israelites from slavery and so he *alone* is to be worshiped (monolatry). This command preps the Israelites for the next stage of their journey—when they enter the land of Canaan with its own lineup of deities, like the storm and war god Baal and the fertility goddess Asherah (mentioned all over the place, especially in 1 and 2 Kings).

The First Commandment is Israel's prime directive: worship only Yahweh. With all the other divine options out there, it's easy to forget.

The Second Commandment drives the point home even further: bowing down before (worshiping) any idols would make Yahweh *jealous* (Exod. 20:4–5). Idols were mainstays of the ancient world, statues of stone, wood, or clay that represented the gods, reminding mortals that the gods, though far off somewhere, were never so far off that they could be forgotten.

Worshiping these idols would make Yahweh *jealous*. Not "What a dumb thought. Please get over the 'idol' idea immediately," but, "Worshiping idols makes me jealous."

Resist entertaining memories of the high-school dating scene. God's jealousy isn't a petty, pouting, brooding kind of resentment or bitterness because your dream guy, whom you'll love till the day you die, doesn't know you're alive and asked someone else to the county fair. God's jealousy is more like what a spouse might feel if the other breaks the marriage vow—which is why worshiping other gods is sometimes depicted in the Old Testament as adultery.

My main point, however, is that for Yahweh to be jealous about sharing his people with other gods, all concerned parties need to be operating on the same assumption, namely, that Yahweh actually *has* something to be jealous about. If my wife were to take a weeklong vacation knitting scarves on an island for grandmotherly women, spousal jealousy wouldn't enter my mind—I'd probably welcome the challenge to see how long I could live on Entenmann's,* Wendy's, and Maker's Mark. But if she announced she was taking off for a month to live in a shirtless under-thirty male colony, I'd have a different reaction.

I'll cross that bridge if and when I come to it. All I want to say here is that Yahweh is deemed worthy of worship not because he is the only God and the Israelites have no other options, but because he isn't and they do. *This is how the Israelites imagined their God*, as the best in a world of many gods.

The stories of Mesha, the plagues, and the first two commandments aren't the only places in the Bible where the "one God among many gods" idea shows up, but they will have to do.** Let me simply sum up by saying that the biblical authors speak of God in ways that reflect their experience in a world where many gods are a given. They are processing their experience of God through the limitations of *their* world.

---

* Have you noticed the prices have been going up while the portions have been getting smaller? Me too.

** If this idea jazzes you, the Psalms are great places to see it, like Psalm 95:3 (*Yahweh is a great God, and a great King above all gods*). Similarly, Psalm 82 (among others) and Job 1–2 portray God as something like a CEO of a "heavenly court" of divine beings—*sons of God* as they are called. Some form of the "one God among many gods" idea even peeks out at us from the New Testament, when Paul writes, *In fact there are many gods and many lords—yet for us there is one God* (1 Cor. 8:5–6). Welcome to the ancient world of the Bible.

And with that we should be very careful to avoid two extremes. The first is looking down on this ancient view of God as simply "wrong." The other is elevating this view off the pages of history, of taking it as timeless and "correct" because it's in the Bible.

We respect these sacred texts best not by taking them as the final word on what God is like, but by accepting them as recording for us genuine experiences of God for the Israelites and trying to understand why they would describe God as they do. God met the ancient Israelites on their terms, in their time and place, stepping into their world.

We follow the lead of these writers not by simply reproducing how they imagined God for their time, but by reimagining God for ourselves in our time, which for us (as we'll get to later) includes taking into account the Christian story as well. In doing so, we will *necessarily* commune with God differently with respect to those who went before.

The ancient ways the Bible describes God drive us to work through what God is like for our own time and place. And, as I've been saying, that process is an act of wisdom, of asking, "What is God like? What God do we truly believe in?"

Paradoxically, that most lofty and honored of questions about the boundless Creator can only be asked by embracing the bounded human conditions of past and present from which these questions spring.

Tiptoeing Around the Touchy Almighty

I mentioned earlier that every issue we've looked at thus far—what to do with a fool, how to look at wealth, how to rear children, how to obey laws, and what God thinks of Nineveh and eating sour grapes—are really about what God is like and what it means to live a life aligned with this God. We are really only dipping our toes in a deep reservoir of examples from the Bible, and we'll definitely be taking a closer look at some other factors later in the book.

But before we move on, I want to circle back to one particularly problematic portrayal of the biblical God that has given the faithful fits and that everyone seems to be talking about these days, especially since 9/11.

In the Bible we see a lot of bloody physical violence that God either commits, commands others to do, or silently watches as they do. That violence can take many forms, but mass killing, sending plagues, and starving people are among the most common and can be inflicted on anyone including God's own people, the Israelites.

Here is my list of the top ten in the order in which they appear in the Bible, though there are others you should feel free to add.

1. God drowns all life on earth except a core few (Gen. 6).

2. God threatens to "consume" (with fire) the Israelites after they build a golden calf (an idol) while Moses was on Mt. Sinai getting the Law. Moses intercedes and convinces God to relent by reminding him that his honor is at stake ("What will the Egyptians say?"). Moses, however, gets the tribe of Levi to go through the camp and kill three thousand of the unfaithful. Yahweh seems pleased, or at least he doesn't comment (Exod. 32).

3. During their forty-year desert wandering, the Israelites are commanded by God to avenge themselves on the Midianites

by killing everyone except the virgin females, whom the men are allowed to divide among themselves (Num. 31).

4. God commands the Israelites to enslave or kill residents of towns along the way to the promised land and simply to kill everything that breathes within the promised land itself, so they can take possession of it (Deut. 7, 20; most of the book of Joshua).

5. According to the long and horrific list of curses we peeked at earlier, upon those who disobey God will bring pestilence, panic, consumption, fever, ulcers, scurvy, grievous boils, madness, blindness, confusion of mind, and sexual abuse. Their crops will fail; their children will be captured. They will be defeated, besieged, reduced in hunger and thirst to cannibalism, and destroyed, scattered among the peoples of the earth (Deut. 28:15–68).

6. While exterminating the Canaanites at God's command, Joshua, among other acts, tracks down five kings, kills them, and then hangs (impales) them on trees (Josh. 10:26).

7. As punishment for an earlier incident in Exodus 17, King Saul wages war against the Amalekites, killing their king, Agag; every man, woman, and child; and the livestock (1 Sam. 15:1–9).

8. As punishment for false worship, God brings the Babylonians to slaughter the Judahites in the streets, leaving their bodies as food for birds and reducing the survivors to cannibalizing their children and neighbors (Jer. 7, 19).

9. Some Psalm writers ask God to slay their enemies, including dashing Babylonian *little ones* against a rock (Ps. 137:9).

10. In the book of Job, God allows a member of his heavenly court, "satan" ("the adversary"), to kill Job's children and livestock and to inflict incredible pain on Job (Job 1–2).*

Struggling with God's violence is nothing new for people of faith. Jews and Christians over the centuries have had to face it frequently, and I'm not sure if there is any part of the biblical story that puts the question "What is God like?" before us today with more urgency and discomfort. After all, these stories are in plain sight, and they don't mince words. Even if we don't acknowledge it consciously, somewhere deep down we are saying either one of two things: "This too I believe about God," or "This I do not believe about God."

Precisely here it is good—actually, a relief—to remember that how any of us, including the biblical writers, see God is inextricably connected to our human experience.

The Israelites didn't make up this notion of divine violence. In fact, in other, older, ancient cultures we know of, violence is woven into the fabric of creation itself: the cosmos was formed after a cosmic battle, where the god who emerged victorious reigned supreme. Such conflict doesn't make it into the creation story in

---

* As a special bonus, here is number 11. After the Israelites complained about the bland diet of manna (bread from heaven) in the wilderness, God sent them quail—three feet deep. But just when they started to eat them, *the LORD struck the people with a very great plague* (Num. 11:31–35).

Genesis 1.* Still, it is no surprise that violence and retribution describe the God of Israel, given the religious climate.

Of course, the gods, like human kings, could also be kind and merciful; they're not just wrath machines. Likewise, the God of the Bible is portrayed in diverse ways. But that doesn't neutralize the fact that one of those ways is as a harsh monarch so typical of the Iron Age world of tribal conflict.

To expect anything else of the biblical writers is to deny their humanity, which—for those who believe God is involved in all of this—God clearly wasn't interested in doing.

As I mentioned earlier, whatever it means to speak of the Bible as inspired by God clearly doesn't mean the Bible is scrubbed clean of the human experience of the writers. And taking seriously the historically shaped biblical portrayal of a violent God drives us to ask for ourselves, "Is this what God is like?"

Ancient biblical writers were already asking that question, as we saw with the story of Jonah and God's about-face concerning the Ninevites. That writer's answer to "What is God like?" was different from Nahum's and from what Israelites had been thinking for who knows how long beforehand. Likewise, the curses of Deuteronomy don't reflect what God is now and always like, but reflect the harsh realities of Judah's political struggles with the Assyrians.

Again, it is superficial to label these violent portrayals of God in the Bible as either "wrong" or "right." They were right for at least

---

* In Genesis 1 God simply speaks and things are. That being said, we do see echoes of a "creation conflict" in several places, like Psalm 89:10, where Yahweh *crushed Rahab like a carcass*, and Psalm 74:13–14, where God *broke the heads of the dragons* and *crushed the heads of Leviathan*, all of which depict God's defeat of the sea at creation in a manner reminiscent of Mesopotamian and Canaanite stories where the sea is depicted as a serpent or dragon.

some of the ancient Israelites working within the cultural horizons that defined the nature of reality and of the gods. The question of right or wrong only comes up when we expect from the Bible timeless, unchanging facts about God.

To put it another way, the problem of divine violence becomes far less of a problem when we remember *why* some biblical writers portray God violently. They are making sense of God with the ancient vocabulary available to them in their world. And like most things in the Bible, God is presented in diverse ways along with the changing experiences of the ancient Israelites and then the first followers of Jesus.

* * *

In case I haven't been as clear as I think I've been, let me say for the record that I don't believe that the God of galaxies, light-years, and dark matter fights battles with other gods or has heavenly board meetings, or that other gods exist that can effectively be appeased by child sacrifice to win local skirmishes. Nor do I believe God passes out violent retribution like he's sowing grass seed. I *do* believe that the Israelites at some point believed these things about God. They imagined God in the only way that God would make sense to them—through the language and concepts of their time and place.

Such imagining of God isn't a problem to be solved. We all do that. We can't help it. And that tells us something about the nature of the faith and the role the Bible plays in our journey of faith.

But now, let's bring Jesus into this, at least a bit.

Chapter 8

Interlude: Jesus and All That

God Is _____ (Fill in the Blank)

The Bible does not leave us with one consistent portrait of God, but a collection of ancient and diverse portraits of how the various biblical writers understood God for their times. These biblical portraits of God are not there to test how clever we can be in making them all fit together nicely. They illustrate for us the need to accept the sacred responsibility of asking what God is like for us here and now.

We can hardly turn a page of the Bible without seeing God imagined as a king, shepherd, rock, fortress, vine, or potter. God isn't actually any of those things (obviously), but those ways of depicting God reflect the "givens" of an ancient culture that drew tribal boundaries, farmed, tended animals, and made their own pottery. It's like when eighteenth-century philosophers and theologians referred to God as a "divine watchmaker." Generations of smartphone and smartwatch users will come up with their own analogy.

At any rate, images of God as a potter or king, though relatively innocent, are no less culturally conditioned images of God than are "Yahweh is the best God among all the gods" or "Yahweh tends to solve conflicts through violence." They all reflect the cultural language used for God at the time.

How else could these people of faith talk about God? How else could *anyone* talk about God? Who we are and when and where we exist affect how we imagine God.

Whenever we say to ourselves, "Well, that's true, but *of course* God is _____," we should pay attention to how we fill in that blank. It will tell us a lot about how we imagine God in our here and now. Even something that seems *really* obvious and not culturally bound at all, like "God is love," is loaded with all sorts of ready-made ideas about what we mean when we say the word.

The ancient Israelites saw Yahweh's love as his steadfast commitment to them, keeping his promises, holding up his end of the bargain—"faithfulness" to an agreement is a good way of putting it; God's "love" is like that of a good king committed to the welfare of his people. For us, though our ideas of God's love may include something like that, it tends to be more individualistic, personal, and emotional than how ancient Israelites thought of God. And for Christians, of course, how we imagine God's love is deeply affected by God's act of self-sacrifice—Jesus's death on the cross. It's unlikely, however, that ancient Israelites would have considered such a shameful death as an act of God's love.

All this makes me wonder at what point are we *not* reimagining God in ways that fit our here and now? Don't we all go beyond what the Bible says and imagine God for ourselves? Whether we realize it or not, isn't that happening all the time? I think it is.

Rather than recoiling at the thought, we should embrace, as we've seen, the fact that reimagining God is modeled for us within the Bible itself. Do we really think we are so above the fray of the human drama that we can avoid it? Maybe that is exactly what God wants.

In fact, what is the story of Jesus and the Good News if not a re-imagining of the "God of the Bible"?

It's What Christians Do

Jesus's crucifixion, for example, represents a major reimagining of God. Child sacrifice for Israelites is condemned in no uncertain terms in the Old Testament. It is abhorrent and listed as one of the abominations committed by King Manasseh (whom we met earlier) that led to the exile. And yet central to the story of Jesus is God the Father doing that very thing while at the same time turning the idea of Old Testament sacrifice on its head. Now God is the one offering a sacrifice for humanity rather than humans sacrificing to God, as it always was.

What's going on here? Is this God up to something new? Yes.

The New Testament writers did not reject the God of the Old— they reimagined God, because the gospel in their time and place demanded it. The God-language of their Jewish tradition could not fully account for what the (Jewish) New Testament writers believed God had done in Jesus of Nazareth in their time.

The same goes for the resurrection. This was off script. Not only was the idea of people rising from the dead in general not really a thing in the Old Testament,* but the notion that Israel's king would alone be raised from the dead after being executed by another power

---

* Daniel 12 is the lone exception, which biblical scholars typically consider to have been written in the second century BCE. But in the Old Testament in general, bodily resurrection wasn't part of the script. The New Testament idea owes more to postexilic Judaism than it does to the Old Testament, which is a big topic we'll come back to in chapter 12.

was utterly and completely unexpected—ridiculous, in fact. Yet, this is what Jesus followers believed God did.

And so God had to be reimagined.

No one struggled with this more than the apostle Paul, who pored over his Bible to find creative ways to connect Israel's story with this unexpected turn in Jesus.

Paul preached that God *no longer* required of God's people circumcision or strict dietary observances, even though both are nonnegotiable commands of God in the Old Testament (Gen. 17; Lev. 11; Deut. 14). Gentiles who trust in Jesus are now also fully "children of Abraham" without needing to obey first these ancient divine commands that had formerly defined what "children of Abraham" meant.

Paul reimagines God to account for his here and now, which is that Jesus, the crucified and risen Son of God, has come to save all people, Jews and Gentiles alike.

The idea of reimagining God as times and circumstances change should, therefore, not strike us as odd or the least bit troubling—our Bible is full of reimagining. Without it, there wouldn't be a "New" Testament or a Christian faith tradition. The entire history of the Christian church is defined by moments of reimagining God to speak here and now.

That's what theologians do.

That's what preachers do.

That's what Christian pilgrims do as we journey through life.

Reimagining the God of the Bible is what Christians do. More than that, they *have to,* if they wish to speak of the biblical God at all.

And yes, that is yet another paradox—the God of old can only be accessed by being reimagined. Judging from the fact that this has been happening all along, even going back to the pages of the Bible itself, I'd like to make the rather bold suggestion that God is okay with it.

At least I hope so, for we humans can never jump out of our skin and see things from above. We only see from below. And I count it a blessing, not a problem, when I see that the biblical writers did that for themselves, and that move has continued throughout the long histories of Jewish and Christian thought.

Can we really escape this same responsibility? Should we even want to?

Does Your God Recycle?

Should we be the least bit surprised when we, along with some biblical writers, find ourselves wandering beyond the words in the Bible as we think about what God is like, sensing that the God we see there made sense for that time but not necessarily for ours, and that the God we were introduced to in the Bible is not in every way the God we believe in here and now?

My answer to that rather convoluted question is, "No, we should not be surprised." God is relentlessly reimagined all around us. American Christians have reimagined God as feminist, environmentalist, capitalist, refugee, soldier, Republican, Democrat, socialist, and on and on. Some portraits of God I agree with more than others (and let the debates begin), but the act of reimagining God in ways that reflect our time and place is self-evident, unavoidable, and necessary.

When the situation was dire, the ancient Israelites expressed their hope in God in ways that needed to be heard at the time—in pleas for economic justice, integrity of their leaders, success against their enemies. The questions for us, as they have been for all generations, are:

> What is *our* hope?
>
> How do *we* yearn for God to show up here and now?
>
> What urgent thing is happening right now to *us*, our families, and our world?
>
> What *new* thing will the God of *old* do now?

These are the questions driven by wisdom that we ask ourselves as the biblical writers did ages ago.

When I see God presented today as a champion of the full equality of women, people of color, refugees, or the environment, I say, "Yes, this is my God too. This is the God I believe in."

But this is a reimagined God.

As hard as it might be to hear, the God of the Bible, strictly speaking, doesn't actually champion these causes, however important they might be to us. If biblical writers could listen in to our God-talk, they might not recognize their God in what we say, at least not without some prompting.

Sure, we might see hints in the biblical story where something like "God sides with refugees" can find a hook, and for some issues that hook is bigger than others (the justice and fairness hooks are huge, for example). *But the biblical hook is brought in after the fact.* The actual feeling of compassion for refugees doesn't begin by reading the Bible. Rather, the Bible comes into the picture afterwards as a way of grounding that compassion in our faith tradition.

We find in the Bible ways of anchoring our experience of God—

even if that means reading the Bible in fresh and creative ways, which is exactly how we see the New Testament writers engaging their Bible when they talk about Jesus.

We're getting a little bit ahead of ourselves, and we'll come back to this shortly. For now let me just repeat that this process of reimagining God is not a problem to be overcome, but an invitation to meet the always active, always present God here and now, where we are, and to trust that God is with us in that process.

By saying, "*This* is my God," I am accepting the responsibility of our inevitable task of finding those sacred places where God and our world meet. This is why I disagree with Christians who say, for example, that women are not permitted to have leadership roles in churches or Christian organizations. I understand that there are Bible verses that might preclude women from preaching or teaching men (which we'll come back to), but simply lifting those verses out of the Bible without further ado is in my opinion to relinquish the sacred responsibility of reimagining God for our here and now.

I can certainly understand why some might say that Christian faith and practice should not depend on the demands of our current pagan, secular, very unchristian culture. Fair enough. But if you throw down that card too quickly, it will backfire.* The ancient world, after all, gave us warring gods and heavenly board meetings. *If that doesn't fit the definition of "pagan influence," I don't know what does.* And yet ancient Israelites imagined God within that world—*and those images became part of our sacred scripture.*

I think it's worth sitting with that last thought and pondering it for a moment.

---

* Mixed metaphor. Just seeing if you're paying attention.

The Creator is being reimagined all the time and can be reimagined through the lens of *any* culture, of *any* time and place. No one culture, and certainly not the (largely white male affluent) Western culture I inhabit, can claim superior status for reimagining God once and for all. The Creator doesn't need any of us to sit atop the mountain and speak down to everyone else.

Perhaps this is at least one reason why the Christian faith has had such staying power and spread broad and wide—different people living in different times and places can connect with this God in ways that engage their world and make sense to them.

* * *

We are not the first, prompted by the time and place of our existence, to ask "What is God like?" But the question remains whether we accept the responsibility to answer that question. And we are not turning away from scripture (or God) when we do so, but turning toward scripture as it models that very process.

All of which is to say, God is out ahead of us leading us on. We only need to follow.

This is the God I choose to believe in, the one I imagine, a God who is quite aware of the fact that we cannot help when and where we were born, but remains with us just the same and encourages us to accept the challenge of owning our faith here and now rather than relinquishing that sacred responsibility by expecting others to have done it for us.

And when we do that, we are joining an ancient conversation, and once we hear it, we'll wonder how we hadn't noticed it before.

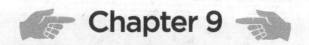

Chapter 9

Seriously Updating the Ancient Faith

Adapting to Survive

I have all my computer software and operating-system updates set on automatic. I don't want to think about the updates; I just want them to happen. I figure there are some competent Apple nerds out there who do nothing but stay up nights patrolling the internet searching out and destroying threats, foreign and domestic. There are people out there, equally nerdy, likely working out of their mom's basement in some faraway place where they don't have laws, who are also staying up nights thinking of new ways to invade and destroy my little cyberecosystem. As the bad guys keep adapting, so does Apple. It's a matter of survival.

Speaking of survival, more literally, I also get a yearly flu shot. I'm never really sure exactly what type of flu I'm being vaccinated for—is it the throwing-up kind or the coughing-up-a-lung kind? Or is throwing up not a flu thing? I forget. And how different is a flu from a really bad cold? But I get the shot anyway, not only for the neat "You Did It!" sticker, but because whatever a flu is (and please don't send me hundreds of emails explaining the difference), I don't want it.

Those little viruses are *so clever*! They find all sorts of ways to adapt to last year's vaccine, because those buggers are determined to give me whatever it is they give me. I'm not sure why they are so highly motivated, though I imagine it has to do with their wanting to survive too—which is fine, but I'd rather they do it somewhere else, like my neighbor's four dogs that bark nonstop or the mice that keep building a nest inside my lawn tractor.* But they adapt, alarmingly quickly, and the vaccines have to keep up, or else I'm going to feel like crap.

I guess when you stop to think about it, most things adapt. I don't mean coming out with a new version of something just because it will sell and shareholders need to be kept happy (once again, Apple), but adapting as a matter of survival. Blockbuster famously didn't adapt and now look at it. You can't. Blockbuster is as dead as pagers and typewriters. Companies that have an eye on market changes survive by reinventing themselves, like every electronics powerhouse that saw the writing on the wall for boom boxes when music went digital.

And of course, there's always McDonald's and Taco Bell, changing their menu every six months to keep people walking through the door. I'm not sure how many people turn to Taco Bell for their vegetarian option, nor to McDonald's to grab their side salad or a gourmet coffee (that tastes like swill). Only time will tell, though while we're waiting I'm sure their boards of directors are driving very nice cars and living in very nice houses.

Even life adapts, if you're into evolution and that sort of thing. According to some cable show I watched, the only reason we human beings are here is because dinosaurs, after a rather hefty 160-million-

---

* Suburban problems.

year run, suddenly went extinct about 66 million years ago due to (as the theory goes) a massive meteor that hit the Yucatan Peninsula causing darkness and massive climate change to sweep over the earth. We are here today because some mammals of the burrowing variety survived by going underground and, when the all-clear signal was given, emerged and adapted. So, thank you, meteor, and thank you, furry little rodent-type things.

Religious traditions adapt too—for survival. That could mean suburban churches introducing clowns and coffee bars in the foyer to attract more people to cover the budget. Or it can mean another type of survival—a more serious one—that characterizes both Judaism and Christianity since . . . well . . . forever: the need to pass on the religious tradition from generation to generation.

That has *always* involved some sort of adaptation—some adjustments or changes, something new that was not done or thought of before.

And so we are back to our paradox: to maintain any tradition, you *need* to hold on to some aspects of the past *while at the same time* thinking creatively about how the past and the present can meet— reimagining the faith, as I've been putting it. The perennial wisdom question is, "What remains and what gets transformed?"

At what point have we left the tradition by adjusting it to the present, and at what point have we killed the tradition by refusing to change at all? Addressing those questions describes the entire history of Judaism and Christianity, beginning already within the pages of the Bible itself and through to this very moment.

To honor tradition means adapting that tradition in order to keep it vibrant. It may seem totally counterintuitive, but you can't really honor a tradition unless you are willing to change it. Survival is at stake.

Standing on a Table Covered in Syrup with My Hair on Fire

Judaism has had a roughly three-thousand-year history, which is remarkable. I think God has something to do with this, but practically speaking Judaism survived because it has adapted its sacred tradition to its ever-changing environment while at the same time maintaining the tradition.

Or maybe we can give that a little more punch: Judaism was faithful to its tradition *by* adapting that tradition *so that it could survive*. Not in a willy-nilly, let's-throw-caution-to-the-wind sort of way, but Judaism adapted nonetheless—or risked letting the tradition die altogether.

To think of either the faith of the Old Testament Israelites or the Judaism that emerged after the Babylonian exile as rigidly orthodox and unyielding to change simply isn't true.

We've already glimpsed some of these adaptations of the old ways: the slave and Passover laws were given different meaning over time; 2 Chronicles radically reinterpreted the reign of Manasseh in order to speak to Jews living in a new time and place; Jonah's view of outsiders flipped what Nahum thought.

This process of needing to adapt over time—as I will not tire of emphasizing—is *part of the biblical fabric, baked into its pages, and a crucial yet overlooked aspect of the Bible's character as a book of*

wisdom rather than a once-for-all book of rules and static information.
The Bible in that respect is more like a living organism than a
carved tablet.

And thank goodness for that, because any other kind of Bible
would have been dead on arrival within a few decades of when it
was written. The viability of the Christian faith too—as we will see
in more detail later—rests on the New Testament writers creatively
adapting the story of Israel to account for Jesus. They did nothing
less than reimagine God, a pattern that long preceded the Christian
faith and that continued to be used by that faith in the millennia that
followed.

Adapting the past for the present is a wisdom move. Preserving
faith in God is not about sticking to the past no matter what, but
always asking anew how the past and the present can coexist.

But, forgive me, we're getting a bit ahead of ourselves again. Back
to Judaism.

One early biblical hint of the type of reimagining we are looking
at concerns the "one God among many" idea we looked at earlier.
That biblical portrait of God, as you will recall, reflected the religious
culture of the time, where gobs and gobs of gods filled the heavens.
Well before the time we get to Jesus and Paul, however, Judaism became monotheistic. Gone were the days of Yahweh doing battle with
the gods of Egypt or Moab. Though Paul's heavens were active with
supernatural entities (Eph. 6:4; 1 Cor. 8:5), only one was worthy of
the title "God."

How that transition happened is one of the puzzling features of
ancient Judaism, and it won't be solved here. We have the Old Testament uncomfortably assuming that other gods exist, and then when

we turn to the time of the New Testament, it's as if we're looking in on another world entirely—which we are. We do see some movement, though, in a few Old Testament stories.

For example, in one section of the book of Isaiah, written in the wake of the exile, we read: *I am the first and I am the last; besides me there is no god* (44:6). For this prophet, idols are frauds, inanimate objects made by ironsmiths and carpenters, useless lumps of wood suited only for cooking food or keeping warm (44:12–20).* Jeremiah, another prophet of the exile, uses similar language about idols (10:1–18). In the entertaining story in 1 Kings 18:20–40, the prophet Elijah** teases and mocks the priests of the Canaanite god Baal when their god does not show up for a divine duel with Yahweh. At one point Elijah even suggests that perhaps Baal needed to use the restroom, which is to say he isn't a god at all. I'm not kidding. *He has wandered away* in verse 27 is a euphemism for going potty.

We are not yet in the world of full-blown monotheism, though we are moving in that direction, and the experience of exile seems to have played some role in this shift in thinking.

---

* The prophet Isaiah lived in the late eighth century BCE. Isaiah 44:6–20, however, is part of a section of Isaiah beginning in chapter 40 that biblical scholars date to the sixth century (or later), because the Babylonian exile is already assumed to have happened. This so-called Second Isaiah—which may have been an individual or more likely a "school" of followers—carried forward anonymously the tradition of the great eighth-century prophet.

** The stories of the kings of Israel in 1 and 2 Kings were also written and edited around the time of the Babylonian exile. The *events* that biblical books describe don't tell us when the book was *written*—which if you think about it is not a very daring idea. Historical novelists do this all the time. Nathanial Hawthorne didn't live in the seventeenth century Massachusetts Bay Colony and yet he wrote *The Scarlet Letter*.

If I stood on a table covered in syrup with my hair on fire, I still couldn't draw enough attention to the importance of the Babylonian exile for the Israelites' reimagining of God in the centuries that followed.

Living on Babylonian soil was a new "here and now" that had to be addressed. Seeing their capital city and Temple razed and being deported to a foreign land were more than an inconvenience. With no land, no king, and no Temple and surrounded by the religious practices of their captors, Israelites surely thought God had finally abandoned them. This raised all sorts of questions in people's minds, namely, "Was all this trust in Yahweh worth it?" "Does this God want anything to do with us or has he turned his back forever?" "Is this even the true God?"

The harsh realities of changing times and nothing less than an unraveling social-religious fabric raised new questions that their ancestors never dreamed of—or if they did, those questions would now take on a practical urgency like never before. Modes of thinking from a more sheltered past were not adequate for dealing with this catastrophe.

The Israelites had to adapt to a different world. One of those adaptations, a fundamental one, has been staring us in the face all along.

We Need to Get This in Writing

Before the Judahites returned from exile, there was no "Bible," nor would there be such a book for some time to come. To be sure, back in the days of the monarchy the ancient Israelites began keeping records of various sorts—like kingly activities, laws, stories of the deep past, and other things. That is how the Bible began—or better, these were the early writings that would eventually make up parts of the Bible.

We see hints of this process in the stories of Israel's kings (1 and 2 Kings). For example, the story of the reign of Jeroboam, the first king of the north, ends (as they all do) with his death and this notice: *Now the rest of the acts of Jeroboam, how he warred and how he reigned, are written in the Book of the Annals* of the Kings of Israel* (1 Kings 14:19). Likewise, the book of Numbers mentions a catalogue of battles called *the Book of the Wars of the LORD* and cites it in 21:14–15.

This is as close as the Bible gets to footnotes. A written tradition was already under way, and it would eventually be adapted and woven into the stories we see in the Bible.

But a Bible—the kind of sacred book we take for granted in our very literate and bookish world—did not exist. That was an innovation that grew out of the crisis of exile.

One big clue that the Bible came along later is how little the stories of the kings and the prophets look back to the time of Moses or quote the Law of Moses, even when the topic calls for it. Though Moses and his story were likely known, in some form, there was no officially sanctioned book to appeal to. There were laws, but there was no Pentateuch, no Torah (Hebrew, meaning "teaching"), that served as a recognized compendium of ancient commands by which kings were judged.

For example, given that many of the kings of Israel were guilty of breaking the first two commandments (worshiping other gods or

---

* Do not make the mistake some of my college students do and spell this word with one *n*. Annals are official year-to-year court records. With only one *n* we have a very different word, indeed.

making idols), one might expect now and then something like, "As the LORD commanded Moses on Mt. Sinai," or words to that effect. But no. They mention royal annals and books of war, but not Genesis or Leviticus.

What the Bible (or proto-Bible) looked like at the time of David, or Josiah, or the exile, and so on are open questions. However we might try to answer those questions, which have occupied biblical scholars for centuries, we only need to see that the Bible as we know it today wasn't always part of the life of ancient Israel. It was created and *became* part of their life, however, when the *need* arose—with the effective removal of God's presence from the people in the exile and the centuries to follow.

Creating a book that recounted and evaluated the past and gave a vision for the future addressed a pressing need brought on by a dramatic and devastating turn of circumstances. Creating a Bible—compiling and editing older stories and writing some new ones—was an effort to remain connected to the past amid uncertain times.

Ironically, *the thing that threatened ancient Israel's existence, the exile, is what led to the creation of a sacred book that ensured Israel's survival through the southern kingdom of Judah.* Jews would become the "people of the book," and that book has helped carry their tradition forward much farther than I'm sure any Jews would have imagined some twenty-five hundred years ago—and it hasn't exactly hurt Christianity, either.

On the other hand, "putting it in writing" would also create several metric tons of challenges, all of which can be summed up as follows: once you put the sacred tradition in writing, it is less a living tradition and more locked into a time gone by. As the decades and then centuries passed after the exile, the days of old faded farther and farther back in time. The Jews kept right on going, however, all the while dealing with one foreign landlord after another.

Adapting this inscripturated past for life in the present was inevitable. Different Jewish groups may have had different ideas about *how*, but they all adapted their beliefs and behaviors somehow. They had to.

The few biblical examples that we've seen of adapting the past to new situations aren't random blips on the screen. They are, rather, early stirrings of a phenomenon that will come to occupy Judaism and Christianity throughout their entire histories, asking again and again the wisdom questions we've been looking at, "How can we stay connected today to the tradition of the past? How does there and then speak to us here and now?"

The Bible already bears witness to the fact that people of faith dealt with these questions, and the challenges of merging past and present only continued as the decades and then centuries passed.

And not only was the creation of the Bible an innovation, but the Bible itself experienced its own type of innovation early on in its history—namely, the need to be translated into other languages.

Probably the earliest translation of the Hebrew Old Testament was into Aramaic—something of a close cousin of Hebrew on the ancient language family tree. This translation arose, as all translations do, out of a need.

Hebrew was the language of the Israelites before the exile, but while in captivity they picked up the dominant language of the empire, the international language of politics and trade, Aramaic. It didn't take long before Hebrew was reserved as the language of scribes and other guardians of the tradition, while ordinary people spoke Aramaic. So common was Aramaic that even portions of the

Old Testament, namely, Daniel and Ezra (two postexilic books), were written partly in Aramaic. Aramaic was also, almost certainly, the main language Jesus spoke.

In order for the tradition to survive, a change had to be made—and a big one at that. The language of Abraham, Moses, David, *and God* had to be translated. And no language translates perfectly into another. You always lose something in the translation, even though, as languages go, Aramaic and Hebrew were very similar Semitic languages.*

But a bigger shift was on the way, thanks to Alexander the Great's conquest of the major portion of the Mediterranean world in 332 BCE, which introduced to an already tired people a very different kind of language, Greek, which has no connection whatsoever to Hebrew or any other Semitic language, and boasted a very different kind of culture, one that brought with it some very pressing religious challenges to the Jews.

We are about to see some serious adjustments to the ancient Jewish faith. Again, survival was at stake.

Dealing with an Inconsistent (and Somewhat Ridiculous) God

Greeks were pretty sophisticated, intellectually speaking. They invented philosophy, geometry, science, and democracy, and they did

---

* I'm throwing this in for free. "Semitic" comes from the name Shem, one of Noah's three sons who survived the flood (Gen. 9:18; 11:10–26). His line of descent led to Abraham, the father of Israel. In Hebrew, the consonants *sh* and *s* are almost identically written and were sometimes interchangeable. Hence, "Semitic," meaning of the family of Abraham, or Jewish.

pretty well for themselves in the areas of art and architecture. These were the people who moved into the Jewish neighborhood.

Of course, the Greeks weren't from another planet. Like Jews and other peoples of the time, they had their own religious beliefs and rituals for connecting with the divine realm. But unlike Jews, this didn't keep the Greeks from calculating the curvature of the earth, proposing the existence of atoms, explaining the physical world around them in terms of natural causes, building aqueducts, or discussing whether humans have free will or if everything is predetermined.

We can well imagine Jews feeling a bit out of their element—maybe intimidated and shamed by their own story, which began in slavery, ended in exile, and with absolutely zero contributions to philosophy or science.

"Some 'chosen people'! What kind of God did you say you follow? Apparently one who lets bad things happen to you."

The sacred story of their people and the God they worshiped were becoming something of a problem. God had to be defended, and that meant God had to be reimagined.

For one thing, Greek philosophers thought the idea somewhat ridiculous that the Greek gods were as humanlike as the old myths made them out to be—they lived on a high mountain and held meetings; they had bodies, petty emotions, vindictive behaviors, and uncontrolled sexual urges. You could hardly blame Jews for being somewhat self-conscious and defensive about how similarly humanlike their God appears in their sacred text—Yahweh has a body, gets angry and vindictive quickly, changes his mind, and moves about from place to place as any creature does, and so forth.

I think of Christians who, having been raised to read the Genesis creation story as literal science and history, leave for college, watch the History Channel, or log onto the internet, and find out that fossils and radiometric dating are in fact not hoaxes. That's how nice Christian college freshmen become atheists by Christmas break. If your faith can unravel that quickly, it's enough to make you question whether your faith is worth the effort at all.

Jews living in the Greek period had similar challenges. They addressed those challenges in a number of ways, one of which is the Greek translation of the Hebrew Old Testament, called the Septuagint.*

Translations are great places for religious groups (ancient and modern) to introduce course correctives to some things that might cause embarrassment.

For example, Genesis 2:2 in Hebrew says that God *finished* the work of creation *on the seventh day*—which if you think about it suggests that God actually did some work on the seventh day and then took the afternoon off. But that would imply that God broke on page one of the Bible his own commandment to do no work on the sabbath. The Greek translators saw the problem and made a minor adjustment: *he finished on the sixth day his works.* Now God doesn't contradict himself. Problem solved.

The Hebrew word for a sacrificial altar, *mizbeach* (miz-BAY-ach), is used pretty much across the board in the Old Testament no matter whose altar it is. The Greek translators, however, liked to use two dif-

---

* Septuagint means "seventy." The name is based on a Jewish legend that six members of each of the twelve tribes (so, seventy-two) were sequestered on an island and miraculously cranked out the translation in short order. The historical truth is more complicated. Greek translations were probably grassroots efforts at multiple locations as the need arose after the Greek conquest. The Hebrew version became more the focus of scribes and learned Jews, whereas the Septuagint became the common, and for some Jews even the authoritative, translation. The New Testament writers almost always relied on the Septuagint, so this is no minor point.

ferent words, depending on whether the altar was Israelite or pagan. That change helped clarify that sacrificing to God is nothing like sacrificing to other gods. Not a bad adjustment for Jews living in Greek polytheistic culture, trying to maintain their identity amid the temples and strange gods all around them.

In Hebrew Exodus 24:10 says rather casually that Moses and a party of more than seventy Israelites *saw the God of Israel*, which is a problem because no one is actually supposed to be able to see God. The Greek translation shifts the focus (literally): they *saw the place where the God of Israel stood*. Likewise, after instructions for building the mercy seat atop the ark of the covenant, God says, *There I will meet with you* (Exod. 25:22). In the Septuagint God says, *I will make myself known to you*, which avoids the possibility of God's physically appearing to Moses. And in Numbers 3:16, where the Hebrew refers to God's very humanlike *mouth*, the Greek translation replaces *mouth* with God's *voice*. Yes, humans have voices too, but at least now God doesn't have a body.

The Septuagint really wants to make God seem more, well, godlike.

In Genesis 6:6, which still troubles some readers today, Yahweh says he was *sorry* he created humans; *it grieved him to his heart* (because they kept sinning, which led God to drown everyone). How can someone the Jews claim to be the true God seem so indecisive, not to mention prone to reactive humanlike emotions? So the Greek translation simply gets rid of that idea altogether. Instead of being *sorry*, the Lord *thought deeply*; instead of *grieving*, he *pondered*. Now God is in very Greeklike rational control of the whole process. God isn't taken off guard and doesn't change his mind.

Just to make a point, apparently the ancient Israelites weren't bothered by Genesis 6:6—but we are. We should let that sink in.

Christians today perhaps have more in common with Jews living in a Greek world than we would with the Israelites of the time of David and Solomon. We expect certain things of God and are bothered when we don't see them in the Bible.

Likewise, according to Exodus 4:24, Yahweh is waiting for Moses by the side of the road to—somewhat shockingly—kill him, when he had just gotten done convincing Moses to go back to Egypt and deliver the Israelite slaves. The Greek translation, clearly concerned with such a painful ungodlike about-face, says that *the angel of the* LORD was waiting for Moses. Sure, that doesn't solve the problem entirely, but at least God has a buffer.

These examples illustrate a vital concept for us—Jews at the time changed their sacred text to "clarify" in their time and place *what God is like.* They changed the Bible to accommodate their culture.

All this reminds me of a recent controversy among some Christians, namely, whether Bible translations today should use gender-inclusive language. Talk about a food fight. Whatever one might think of it, the argument that gender-inclusive language is simply "compromising" the Bible for the sake of culture rings rather hollow when we look at what Jews were doing about twenty-three hundred years ago: they produced a culturally influenced Bible translation, the translation that—oh, sweet irony—became the Bible of the New Testament writers.

Another way of handling difficult portions of the Bible was to interpret them in a creative manner called "allegory," which is how sophisticated Greeks also handled their religious literature. Allegory is something of a mindset. It was thought that the true meaning of any literature worth reading lay beyond the literal, surface meanings of mere words, and took on philosophical or symbolic meaning.

Some Jews applied this notion to their scripture. God is infinite and not at all human, and so human words are not adequate for capturing what God is really like. The interpreter's job is to look beyond these mundane words to find the true spiritual message submerged beneath, a message about the virtuous and moral life (a common topic of Greek philosophers).

For example, according to one such interpreter named Philo,* there is more to the "burning bush" incident than meets the eye (Exod. 3:1–6). This is where Moses first meets God, but Philo, in typical allegorical fashion, said that this was no direct encounter with God (since God should not be seeable), but with a go-between—an angel. More important, the burning-but-not-consumed bush wasn't really about God appearing to Moses in the desert. It has, rather, a spiritual meaning: it represents Israel's courageous survival amid terrible suffering (enslavement).

Philo similarly had a problem with God's asking Adam, *Where are you?* after Adam and Eve hid from God for eating the forbidden fruit (Gen. 3:9). Doesn't God know?! He had to ask?! Philo handles this by rephrasing the question as "Where have you arrived, O soul?" meaning something like, "Way to blow it, Adam. Way to not be virtuous. What *have* you done?" Surely, that is what God was *really* saying, wasn't it?

Philo wasn't the only one to defend the faith by adjusting scripture for his time. Another example (a favorite of mine) was the anonymous (probably Alexandrian) writer of the book of Wisdom of Solomon (in the Apocrypha), written to a persecuted Jewish community. This

* Philo (20 BCE–50 CE) was from Alexandria (Egypt), which had been a Greek cultural center and a choice of residence for Jews for centuries. Philo was quite an influential figure in integrating Judaism and Greek culture, and his allegorical method influenced two early Christian theologians, Clement and Origen. This stuff all hangs together, folks.

book is loaded with all sorts of Greek philosophical ideas, like the value of virtue and how the temporary body "burdens" the immortal soul; it generally interprets Israel's history and beliefs in a way that reflects Greek philosophy and not at all ancient Israelite thinking.

Actually, to take a commercial break, one great thing about the Apocrypha is that it was written almost entirely during the Greek period—it's a window onto that period of Jewish history. And now I've gotten you excited about going out and reading the Apocrypha. You're welcome.

The bottom line is that God and the Jewish faith needed some defending, and hellenized ("Greekified") Jews were up for the task of reimagining God. They had to, or risk watching their ancient faith melt away like a snowman on an August sidewalk.

But Jews also had an internal challenge. God's delay in coming to their aid and setting things right for them raised questions of God's justice and goodness. Answering those questions meant reimagining God even more.

God's Honor Is at Stake

"Is God just? Fair? Righteous? Dependable? Steadfast?" These are questions familiar to people of faith across the centuries, including ancient Jews. Given their circumstances—still strangers in their own land, even hundreds of years after the return from Babylon—these were active questions. "What kind of God is this?"

One key way of reimagining God at the time concerns the resurrection of the dead—another thing that Christians may think is more or less fundamental to the biblical package, but that is not the case.

You can read the Old Testament from front to back while standing on your head, and you'll barely get a whiff of the idea that God raises the dead. Yes, it happens. The prophet Elijah revives a widow's dead son (1 Kings 17:17–24). Ezekiel 37:1–14 is a vision of a resurrection, in which dry bones come back to life, a metaphor for Judah's return from exile (see verses 11–14). But I'm talking about people en masse being literally raised from the dead at the end of the world for final judgment by God.

The only place we find that specific idea in the Old Testament is in the book of Daniel: *Many of those who sleep in the dust of the earth shall awake, some to everlasting life, and some to shame and everlasting contempt* (12:2). But that's it. Otherwise the idea of a "general resurrection" for final judgment (as it's called) doesn't appear in the Old Testament—and the one place where it does, Daniel, is a book that doesn't take shape until the second century BCE, right in the middle of the Greek period.

Which brings me to my point: resurrection of the dead was an adjustment to the story, a reimagining of what God will do that arose (an unintended yet fitting pun) during the Greek period to solve a pressing problem that had to do with God's justice and fairness to his people.

What was that problem exactly? A key promise of God to Jews was that faithfulness to God is rewarded; namely, the faithful would take part in the coming restored kingdom of Israel. Two of the three pieces were already in place: they returned to the land after the Babylonian exile and rebuilt their Temple. The missing piece was a king from the line of David reigning from his throne in Jerusalem. Full restoration will be an act of God, God's demonstration of justice and faithfulness to the children of Abraham.

And yet decades and then centuries had gone by with no sign of a Davidic king, during which time—guess what?—faithful and obedient Jews died without seeing the restored kingdom.

While we're on the subject, we see this scenario played out in a more familiar place, Jesus's birth story. In Luke 2:25 we are introduced to Simeon, who was *righteous and devout, looking forward to the consolation of Israel.* Translation: he was an obedient Jew who was hoping that during his lifetime he would see Israel "consoled" or "comforted"—which is straight-up Old Testament language for the return from exile. In fact, the Holy Spirit told him he would. So when he saw the infant Jesus in the Temple and recognized him as *the Lord's Messiah* (verse 26),* he knew that he had seen God's *salvation* (verse 30). The king has come.

At any rate, as if the long wait wasn't hard enough, the Greek period introduced some additional pressing problems that upped the ante considerably: martyrs. Pious Jews were killed for refusing to compromise on God's Law. This came to a head in the early second century BCE. Under the rule of wicked king Antiochus IV Epiphanes (reigned 175–164 BCE), Jews were being coerced to convert to the state-sponsored religion of the Greek empire (supported and encouraged even by some Greek-minded Jewish groups!). Antiochus outlawed Jewish worship, erected in the Jewish Temple an altar to Zeus and an idol of himself—and killed a lot of people.**

---

* *Messiah* is Hebrew for "anointed one," which had become code for "Davidic king." "Christ" is the Greek word for it.

** These persecutions sparked a rebellion that resulted in a brief period of Jewish semi-independence, which is where Hanukkah comes from.

The apocryphal book 2 Maccabees recounts these tense times, no doubt with some literary freedom to make the point vivid. In chapter 7, we read of the gruesome martyrdom of seven brothers and their mother, all of whom were offered the choice to either eat swine's flesh (unclean according to Leviticus 11) or be tortured and killed: scalped, tongues cut out, hands and feet cut off, and fried in a pan. But one after the other they refused, and the response of the second brother to his tormenters gets at why we are taking the time to look at this. Speaking to the wicked king, the brother says:

> *You accursed wretch, you dismiss us from this present life, but the King of the universe will raise us up to an everlasting renewal of life, because we have died for his laws.* (7:9)

The brothers' faith that God will raise them from the dead for being obedient is a huge shift in Jewish thinking, brought about by the difficult reality that God seemed to be taking his sweet old time restoring the kingdom of Israel—centuries, in fact—while Jews were dying for their obedience to God. For God to remain just, for God to remain faithful, something had to give—and what gave was the finality of death. To be just, God would *have* to raise the dead.

Before any of us get the wrong idea, questioning God's justice has a long history for the Israelites. The books of Job and Lamentations and the lament Psalms (like Ps. 89) all take God to task for failing to keep up his end of the bargain to be with his people no matter what.

But now the situation was different. God had to be reimagined to address an unexpected scenario: God's long delay and (apparent) injustice.

When the kingdom finally appears and the golden years of ancient Israel return, God will be faithful to all those martyred Jews: they will be raised from the dead so that they too can take part in the kingdom. Death is not their end. They will *shine like the brightness of the sky . . . like the stars forever and ever* (Dan. 12:3). Or as we see in the book of the Wisdom of Solomon, these righteous immortal souls will *shine forth, and will run like sparks through the stubble. They will govern nations and rule over peoples* (3:7–8).

Resurrection is about God's justice, and God's justice became a more pressing issue than ever before when persecution of faithful Jews abounded and God's absence was painfully felt. How, then, could they maintain their tie with their ancient belief in a just and faithful God amid these dramatically changing circumstances? By reimagining God as someone who *is* just and faithful despite appearances. God now raises the dead.

The biblical script was not prepared to handle such a twist in the story. How could it be?! Adapting the story to the here-and-now realities of life was a wisdom move. What is God like? Is God good and just? Is God faithful? Yes. God must be. And here's how.

Angels and Demons

Angels were not pudgy four-year-olds. They were intimidating heavenly intermediaries between humans and God. It's sort of like the scenario in which you, as a common consumer, have a meeting scheduled with the company president and, instead, you're met in the lobby by his assistant. It's clear that *this* is your meeting. The president is in his high and lofty corner office and you're not going up there.

The Hebrew word for "angel" simply means "messenger," and

angels are certainly known to us in the Old Testament. The big one, of course, is the *angel of the LORD*, who pops in now and then to relay some serious command or bit of news from God. It is this angel who, among other things, kept Abraham from sacrificing his son Isaac (Gen. 22:11) and announced the birth of mighty Samson (Judg. 13:3). Isaiah 6, to give one more example, gives us a glimpse of the heavenly throne of God surrounded by seraphs (fiery angels), each with six wings.

So, we see angelic activity in the Old Testament, but angels become much more active after the exile and in the Greek period. We meet Gabriel and Michael in the book of Daniel* and other named angels, like Uriel and Raphael, in the Apocrypha. Angels seem to have a hand in either writing down the mysteries of God or guiding humans in understanding them—as in Daniel 9. Daniel is concerned why the exile was taking so long, since the prophet Jeremiah said it would only last *seventy years* (Jer. 25:11–12; 29:10). Gabriel answers by letting Daniel in on a little secret: seventy *really* means "seventy sevens," or 490 years.

The reason for this increased prevalence of angels is to make God more accessible. Prophets who relayed God's word to the rest were becoming scarce, a thing of the past, one of the side effects of having God's *written* word. Also, now that God's honor had to be defended, more urgently than in earlier periods, it wouldn't seem right for God to keep popping in and out of the daily and mundane affairs of humans, as Yahweh did when walking and talking with Adam

---

* We also meet them in the New Testament. Gabriel announces to Mary that she is pregnant with Jesus (Luke 1:26). Michael is mentioned in Jude 9 as having a dispute with another new figure, the devil (more below).

and Eve. Other messengers are needed—and the heavenly realm was where they were found.

On the downside, the heavenly realm also included evil beings—fallen angels. Though belief in fallen angels is common among Christians, the chief one being Satan or the devil, the Old Testament doesn't say anything about them. In the New Testament God is said to have consigned some angels to hell (2 Pet. 2:4), but, again, this passage shows the influence of Judaism on the New Testament.

Satan is a word that comes up in the Old Testament, but its meaning shifts as we get closer to the time of Christ. We meet "the satan" in the book of Job (chaps. 1–2), where he is a member of God's "divine council." "Satan" isn't a name here, but a descriptive title meaning "the adversary" or "the accuser." In the book of Job, "the satan" accuses Job of only being pious because he got something out of the deal (a perfect life); he also accuses God of letting Job get away with it. But in Numbers 22:32, for example, the "accuser" is none other than the *angel of the* LORD.

But for Satan as a specific enemy of God (though not yet with the red tights and pitchfork, an image given to us by medieval Christianity), we need to wait for an evolution to occur. The presence of an anti-God figure solved (somewhat) a problem caused ironically by Judaism's deep belief in only one God: Why do bad things happen? Where does evil come from? Who is responsible?

In a world where many gods existed, you could pin horrid events on some erratic divine being. Sure, one of the gods was at the head of the table and ultimately responsible, but they couldn't always be relied on to stay on top of everything. But once you believe that your God is the one and only God, accounting for the presence of evil in the world gets tricky, which philosophers and theologians dutifully call the "problem of evil."

It's a real problem. If God is all-good, all-powerful, and all-knowing and yet bad things happen, might it be that God is none of those things? Blaming human misery on a very powerful divine archenemy keeps God from having to take the blame—though you'd still need to ask why God allows that dark figure to exist, but let's not get sidetracked.

The descriptive title "the satan" of the Old Testament became Satan, the name of this powerful evil being (known also by other names in early Judaism like Mastema and Belial). We see here an adjustment to Jewish thinking that wouldn't have occurred if the need hadn't presented itself. This figure shows up, of course, in the New Testament, as Satan and also the "devil" (from the Greek *diabolos*, meaning "accuser"). That stands to reason, given the fact that the New Testament was written after this development took place.

The Satan we take for granted is a new addition to the ancient tradition. Satan, actually, is a great example of a New Testament "given" that wouldn't exist were it not for the Jewish reimagining of God that went before.

Not Your Father's Judaism

Jewish thinking about God was deeply affected by Greek culture, and we're really just seeing the proverbial tip of the proverbial iceberg.

Christians have said rather freely for almost two millennia that God is all-powerful, all-knowing, and present everywhere at once (omnipotent, omniscient, omnipresent). We do not always realize how completely dependent these ideas are on the ways Greek thought influenced Judaism before Christianity and how ill-fitting these descriptions of God are, biblically speaking.

In the Old Testament, God is not everywhere at once, but moves from place to place, even if one of those places is high above the created order on his heavenly throne. And rather than all-knowing, God clearly sometimes has to find things out.* An all-powerful God is consistent with the Old Testament, where God moves nations and puts the heavenly bodies in their place, but the pressing implications of that wouldn't be felt until the Greek period.

These descriptions of God were introduced under the influence of Greek thought, and yet they came to form the foundation of the language that Christian theologians use to speak of God. We Christians just think of these as biblical concepts, but they are actually tied to how Jews reimagined their ancient God for a new day.

And, as we'll see, reimagining God yet again for other reasons is the heart and soul of the Christian faith.

If we had more time on our hands, we could get into all sorts of other adjustments to the tradition influenced by Greek philosophy: Is life fated, predetermined, by this all-powerful God? Do we have free will? And what happens after we die? Does our body ever come back or are we disembodied souls?

---

* It's hard to get past the story of Adam and Eve and the flood without noticing the misfit of these Greek ideas. For example: God fashions Eve for Adam only *after God realizes* the animals are not "suitable" for Adam; God *takes a stroll* in the Garden of Eden; God *needs to question* Adam after the misdeed; God is *caught by surprise* by humanity's sinfulness and reacts by sending the great flood.

Likewise, we could go on and on about how Jewish society reflected Greek and later Roman ways. The Sanhedrin, a body of Jewish civic leaders who had authority to adjudicate cases, is a Greek idea; the term means "sitting together." A synagogue was a house of prayer and study, and its name was likewise derived from a Greek term meaning "assembly." Both institutions arose as innovations in Jewish life after the exile and are known to us from the New Testament.

Now, I don't want to paint a false picture that every Jew was on the same page when it came to reimagining God for a new time and place. Jews during the Greek and later Roman periods had very sharp disagreements over how best to be faithful to the past in a changing world. How far should they go to adapt to Greek ways? A lot? A little? Not at all? There was no script to follow. Some Jews were quite accommodating to new ways while others held their ground—not unlike the differences among Christians today.

We know from the New Testament and other ancient documents that Judaism sported no fewer than four broad ways ("parties") of addressing the collision of past and present, especially in how to respond to the Roman Empire.

The Sadducees and Pharisees, both prominent in the New Testament, had some rather significant differences in beliefs, including very different attitudes toward their Roman landlords. The Sadducees were more willing to keep the peace with the Roman government that gave them control over the Temple, while the Pharisees, who focused on legal interpretation, were less inclined. The Zealots were keen on overthrowing the Romans by violent means. The Essenes were recluses, sectarians choosing to avoid the conflict by removing themselves from it and waiting it out. (The desert hideout at

Qumran, where the famous Dead Sea Scrolls were found, was probably an Essene community.)

Not all Jews fit into one of these groups (just as not every American is either a die-hard Democrat or Republican today), and there were probably as many options out there as there were neighborhoods. But in a way that's the point—the need to adjust *somehow* to the past in light of the present was universal, if also broad and diverse. They had no script to follow, but they had to do something.

* * *

For the ancient tradition to survive, it had to transform—adapt to changing circumstances. To seek to remain as it always was would simply ensure its isolation, if not its death. The *act* of transformation is, therefore, a sacred responsibility on the part of people of faith in order to maintain that faith. And *how* a tradition is transformed is an act of wisdom.

When we engage that process today, we are simply doing what the Bible itself as well as Jews in the centuries before the time of Jesus had already modeled. Our experiences, what life throws at us, drive us to think about what God is like here and now and consequently what it means to believe in this God. And without making these wise adaptations, however diverse and even conflicting they might have been and regardless of whether some lasted and others didn't, Judaism would not have survived.

And neither would have Christianity.

In fact, it never would have gotten off the ground.

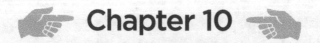

Chapter 10

Treasures
Old and New

German Christmases and French Drains

My parents came to America from Germany in 1956 and brought their German traditions right along with them, a big one being Christmas. We got our stockings on St. Nicholas Day, a full three weeks before the rest of the solar system. I would always find an orange tucked in the bottom. An orange, mind you. I suspect that treasure was a holdover from the old country, when during the war oranges were a special treat. But for me, I never saw the point. I could just walk a few feet into the kitchen and get one myself. What I needed was candy, especially chocolate. Maybe a Matchbox car.

I remember lighting the Advent wreath on each of the four Sundays before Christmas—oh, and those awesome chocolate Advent calendars my grandmother dutifully sent us from Germany! Each day had a cute little door with a piece of chocolate shaped like Santa or something else Christmassy waiting behind it. We also decorated the tree on Christmas Eve and left it up until Epiphany, January 6, which is way later than everyone else. The biggest thing, though, was we Germans opened our presents Christmas Eve after church. I liked that part. Why suffer another twelve hours?

Still, despite my parents' sincere attempts to keep us connected to generations of Germans, those traditions were adjusted in subtle and not so subtle ways in my own family. My wife and I tried, but at the end of the day the only one that made the cut (at least when the kids were young) was lighting the Advent wreath. The first tradition to fall—hard—was presents on Christmas Eve. We decided to be American on that one.

Such is the way of tradition, including the biblical tradition. Some things remain, some are adjusted, and some are discontinued—that uneasy dance between past and present, tradition and change, of feeling grounded through time and yet accepting the need to innovate. And by "biblical tradition" I mean now to turn to the story of Jesus specifically, the gospel, or "Good News," as it's often called.

Christianity was born from the womb of Judaism, and so the story of Jesus the Messiah is deeply and inextricably bound to the story of Israel. But the gospel is also a profoundly creative act—it brings Israel's ancient tradition into a new here and now by (drumroll, please) *adjusting the ancient faith to meet present circumstances*, a process that began within the Old Testament itself.

Judaism during the Greek period, as we've seen, escalated that process. And in the same way Judaism needed to adjust its ancient tradition, the early followers of Jesus needed to continue adjusting that same tradition.

Well, technically, not really "in the same way." Christianity adjusted the tradition in its own and striking ways.

Judaism adapted the past and reimagined God because it had to respond creatively to the unexpected and disastrous crisis of God's abandonment followed by God's centuries-long delay in righting the ship. The early followers of Jesus, though they too engaged the tradition creatively, did so for a very different reason—not because of God's apparent abandonment, but because of God's unexpected, counterintuitive *presence*, namely, in Jesus of Nazareth, a *crucified* Messiah. Such a thing was never part of the playbook of Judaism. To be successful, a Messiah—a chosen, "anointed" leader—should not be executed by Gentiles as a criminal. Messiahs don't lose.

And that's what we are going to be looking at now, how the story of Jesus transforms the ancient tradition and reimagines God. And that reimagining is pretty dramatic, which we will see if we take a moment to step away from the familiarity of it all. The New Testament writers talked about Jesus—paradoxically—as both the true embodiment of Israel's ancient tradition and at the same time a surprising move by God that the tradition did not anticipate.

Or to put it another way, the New Testament writers show us how profoundly new the Good News of Jesus Christ is while at the same time insisting that the story of Jesus is deeply connected to the Jewish tradition that bore and nurtured it.

The New Testament writers faced the challenge of bridging the past tradition and present circumstances, and they did so with a lot of thoughtfulness and creativity.

Which brings us to another pivotal moment in this book—in fact, the big punch line.

Christians throughout time, including today, have had to face that very same challenge of bridging the past and their own unique circumstances. The New Testament, in other words, is our Exhibit A for how vital it is to adjust and reimagine the past to meet the challenges of a new day and time.

That is what Christians do, have always done, and always will do. We are both bound to the past and charged with remaining open to the movement of God's Spirit, which is free and never bound to tradition or our theologies that try to articulate it.

Christian theology, in other words, is an exercise in wisdom—perhaps far more so than is normally thought. We are not simply maintaining the past; we are transforming it, again and again.

And we have *a lot* to learn about this exercise in wisdom from our own Bible, where we see again and again how its writers accepted their sacred responsibility to perceive God's presence for their day in ways that respected the past, but were not bound to reproduce it. As Jesus himself put it, to be *trained for the kingdom of heaven is like the master of a household who brings out of his treasure what is new and what is old* (Matt. 13:52). We are mindful of old treasures, but also anticipate and embrace new ones.

I love that image largely because, as I write this, my basement is in utter chaos with a French drain *and* a new sewer system being expensively installed at the very same ridiculously expensive moment. Before they could start work, my wife and I had to organize the clutter to make room for jackhammers, shovels, and an energetic crew of six. We'd been avoiding the clutter for years, but once we plowed (almost literally) ahead, we came across boxes and boxes of memorabilia from our family's early years—favorite toys and dolls, a Little League score book, children's books, report cards, art projects, notes written to us in oh-so-beautiful childhood cadences.

While working on securing new treasures (a dry basement and the glorious ability to flush our toilets), we found many unexpected old treasures. Both matter. Both are good.

But as Jesus also put it elsewhere, somewhat differently and with a little more punch, *old wineskins* do not have the strength and flexibility to contain the potency of *new wine*. As it ferments, it will *burst* the skins (Matt. 9:17). Translation: the gospel can't be contained in the old ways.

The past is vital, but it's not enough.

In order to account for Jesus, God's surprising move, Israel's story—and even Israel's God—had to be reimagined. If anything, that is what the early Jesus movement was, one big wisdom act of *reimagining God in light of Jesus.*

In fact, the ability to build on the past while at the same time exploding it has allowed the Christian faith to survive across time and cultures. Exactly how the two can coexist is not scripted for us, which is why wisdom must be—and is—front and center. We are, as always, expected to embrace the sacred responsibility of figuring out how to be Christian here and now, respecting the past yet open to the present and future.

Wisdom, in other words, didn't stop being a big deal when Jesus came, as if now finally all answers are given and we can start following the rulebook. Wisdom continues to be fundamental to faith. Jesus and the gospel have more to do with wisdom than we might be used to hearing.

Something About Jesus That Doesn't Get the Attention It Deserves

Jesus is described in all sorts of ways in the Bible—king, prophet, priest, savior, shepherd, door, gate, vine, healer, rabbi, Lord—all of which are fine and good, of course, though some other words tend to get lost in the shuffle. Jesus was also a wise teacher, a sage, a purveyor of wisdom and the deep mysteries of God, a teller of stories, a confounder of the so-called wise.

It has bothered me for some time how little press wisdom gets in the Christian world I inhabit when we see how central it is to the Old Testament. I suppose one reason for this lack is that wisdom gets messy, compared to thinking of the life of faith as a set of rules and clearly defined and never-changing boundaries. We are just people, after all, and we tend to gravitate toward the black and white.

But the Christian faith doesn't.

Think of Jesus's main teaching method: telling parables. If your aim is to get people to comprehend black-and-white information, try a lecture or a press release. If you want to move people to own the moment and take responsibility to work it out for themselves, you tell them a story to stimulate their imagination.

The Gospels record almost forty distinct parables (who knows how many more Jesus told), and not a single one of them has a clear and obvious meaning. And if you think they do, I suggest you walk into a room of eager Bible readers studying a parable, make your case for its obvious meaning, and then duck for cover; or wander into a theological library and go to section BT373 through 378 and start reading. Parables can be downright obscure, so much so that Jesus's own disciples sometimes looked like fourteen-year-old gamers trying to grasp theoretical physics.

And if parables themselves weren't enough of a challenge, Jesus announces his surprising—even disturbing—purpose for using them:

> *To you [the disciples and others close to Jesus] has been given the*
> *secret of the kingdom of God, but for those outside, everything*
> *comes in parables; in order that*

"they may indeed look, but not perceive,
and may indeed listen, but not understand;
so that they may not turn again and be forgiven."
(Mark 4:11–12; Matt. 13:13; Luke 8:10; quoting Isa. 6:9–10)

If I want to prepare my students for an exam—if I want them to grasp the material—I won't tell them cryptic, ambiguous stories without explanation with the intention of keeping them befuddled. Some of my students think that's *exactly* what I do, but they are wrong, and they deserve the grade they get. If Jesus's main goal were to be crystal clear, he wouldn't have introduced thick layers of ambiguities and possible misunderstandings. But that's what he did. Because he is a sage.

Jesus tells us that the kingdom of God (or kingdom of heaven*) is like a mustard seed, a fig tree, a sower sowing seeds, hidden treasure, yeast, wheat, a fishing net, a narrow door, a dinner party, sheep, coins, headstrong children, a widow, a tax collector, and so forth. Jesus was clearly more interested in painting portraits, creating a vision, and overturning conventional thinking. You do that by telling a story that leaves people thinking, uncomfortable, moved, motivated—or in some other way invested.

Careful readers and writers have pondered these parables for two thousand years, offering fresh interpretations along the way. That's

---

* The "kingdom of God" and the "kingdom of heaven" are the same thing. Just be clear that this kingdom isn't *in* heaven, which we may (or may not) enter in the distant future, but here and now—as Jesus prayed, *Your kingdom come, your will be done, on earth as it is in heaven* (Matt. 6:10). The parables aren't instructions for getting into heaven one day, but for living the kingdom life now.

what's so great about parables—they just keep giving, because, just like Proverbs, they are open-ended and ambiguous, inviting us to ponder and then bring their wisdom into our own circumstances.

Parables are meant to have an afterlife, to be flexible, adaptable over time to new circumstances. Parables are how wise teachers incite change, not just for the moment, but at all times and in all places. Including ours.

Another sagely side of Jesus is how he answers questions when challenged by the guardians of the status quo. He rarely if ever goes for a straightforward answer and often answers the question with another question, like this little number from the Gospel of John. Jesus had just announced to the religious leaders that he and his heavenly Father are unified in their purpose—as he puts it, *The Father and I are one* (John 10:30). As they were picking up stones to stone him for blasphemy, Jesus responds in a cool and collected manner that in my opinion borders on snarky: *I have shown you many good works from the Father. For which of these are you going to stone me?* (verse 32). He then goes on to confound and outwit them with a clever interpretation of Psalm 82. The details don't need to detain us here, but just know that he puts his opponents in their place.

Jesus was a clever and crafty debater, as wise master teachers should be. Good teachers can handle any student question, especially if the question is meant merely to catch the teacher off guard and prop up the student's ego. Jesus shuts that down. And yet with the poor and downtrodden Jesus is open and inviting. His method depends on the audience. He "reads the situation," a requirement of wisdom already seen in Proverbs.

Jesus also uses the language of wisdom in his teaching moments, some of which sound as though they could easily have come right out of the book of Proverbs. For example, he speaks of *wise* builders who build their houses on solid rock and *foolish* builders who build their houses on the sand (Matt. 7:24–27). The difference between the two is whether they put Jesus's words into action. Wisdom in Proverbs too is all about listening to wise teaching and acting upon it. Jesus is not about teaching "correct thinking," but realigning minds, hearts, and motivations to act well, to live in harmony with the kingdom of heaven.

Wisdom language really pops up frequently. As a boy, Jesus was *filled with wisdom* and *increased in wisdom* (Luke 2:40, 52). Not only Jesus's teachings, but his miracles are chalked up to wisdom as well: *What is this wisdom that has been given to him? What deeds of power are being done by his hands!* (Mark 6:2). Even his simple act of roaming about the countryside and proclaiming the kingdom is like Woman Wisdom in Proverbs crying out in public places:

> *Wisdom cries out in the street;*
> *in the squares she raises her voice.*
>
> *At the busiest corner she cries out;*
> *at the entrance of the city gates she speaks:*
>
> *"How long, O simple ones, will you love being simple?*
>
> *How long will scoffers delight in their scoffing*
> *and fools hate knowledge?*
>
> *Give heed to my reproof;*

I will pour out my thoughts to you;
I will make my words known to you." (Prov. 1:20–23)

Following Jesus's teachings *is* following the path of wisdom—it is your actions, what you say and do to others, not maintaining a hard-line doctrinal stance or turning faith into an intellectual abstraction. And just like Proverbs, Jesus's teachings are long on casting a vision, but short on scripted details. We have to figure it out every bit as much as we have to work out whether to answer or not answer a fool (Prov. 26:4–5). Following the Sage of Sages takes wisdom and produces wisdom.

The life of faith is a journey alongside the wise master teacher.

Jesus, Wisdom from God

One of Jesus's favorite activities seems to be debating the meaning of Torah with his fellow Jews, normally scribes and teachers, often egged on by them. As we saw in chapter 3, the Law is ambiguous. And so, beginning within the Old Testament itself, Judaism has a long history of debate and deliberation over what individual laws actually require. Those deliberations are examples of a wisdom activity demanded by the ambiguous and ancient nature of biblical laws.

And so when Jesus joins the debate over the meaning of a law, he is not claiming (as Christians sometimes misunderstand) that the Law is a bad thing. He is, rather, doing what Jews have always needed to do, given the ambiguous nature of these sacred laws.

Where Jesus adds something new, however, is in setting himself up as the supreme interpreter of Torah and in doing so claiming to reveal the deeper will and mind of God, which go beyond the words on the page. Jesus holds the Law in one hand and wisdom in the other, because the two go together, as we saw earlier.

True, on Mt. Sinai God *had* said, "Do not murder," "Do not commit adultery," "Divorce only for good reason," "Fulfill your vows," "An eye for an eye" (Matt. 5:21–42). Jesus does not dismiss these commands, but he does take them to a deeper place than where those laws go on their own. And so Jesus says: *You have heard that it was said, . . . But I say to you . . .* Now murder includes hatred, adultery includes adulterous thoughts, the only reason for divorce is adultery, vows of any kind should be avoided, and one should turn the other cheek rather than retaliate.

According to Jesus, God is after our deep inner transformation, in those dark places of the soul, those little and hidden things we keep secret from everyone else. Jesus isn't playing a legalistic game, but through the Law pointing people to a God revealed in Israel's sacred story, but also limited by the "old wineskins."

Jesus interprets the ancient Law for a new day, which we've also seen already: Deuteronomy interprets the slave law of Exodus more justly; Ezekiel marginalizes the older notion that one's actions have intergenerational consequences; the Passover morphs from a family meal at home to a national feast in Jerusalem. All of which is to say that Jesus debates the meaning of biblical laws not to dismiss them, but to see beyond them to the deeper will of God not captured by the script.

Seeing Jesus as the Sage of Sages should perhaps not come as a complete surprise, especially when we glimpse back at how John begins his Gospel. He speaks of the *Word*, who was *in the beginning*, was *with God*, and indeed *was God*. And through the Word came everything that exists, and in the Word is *life* and *light* (John 1:1–4). This divine *Word* then *became flesh and lived among us* (1:14).

"Word" is a concept borrowed from the world of Greek philosophy. The Greek term is *logos*, and grasping its exact meaning can be tricky. It often means something like logic, reason, or divine thought or plan.* In some Jewish circles influenced by Greek thought, "Word" was the divine "force" of creation as well as a divine mediator bridging the gap between God and humans.

It gets a bit abstract, and I don't mind saying that I've never been particularly clear on what John is getting at here, but he is at the very least saying something of considerable importance about Jesus: as the Word with God at creation, Jesus is described in a way that unmistakably echoes the description of wisdom we already saw in Proverbs 8 (especially verses 22, 30) and wisdom's role in creation. And note too that John's *In the beginning was the Word* is meant to get readers to think of the opening words of the book of Genesis, *In the beginning*.

For John "Word" combined the Hebrew notion of wisdom as a basic property of the cosmos and the Greek concept of *logos* current at the time and that Jews were already familiar with. But John's twist—a rather remarkable one at that—is that this divine *logos* becomes flesh rather than a fleshless divine intermediary between God and mere mortals.

And all of that brings me to this: the incarnation—the "enfleshing" of God that we celebrate each Christmas, and which is such a core mystery of the Christian faith—is a rather striking reimagin-

---

* Not to get pedantic about it, but *logos* is derived from the verb *legein* ("to speak") and shows up all over the place in English meaning either "speech," as in "eulogy" (speaking a "good word" of the departed), or a body of knowledge, as in "anthropology," "zoology," and everything in between, including college courses you may have hated.

ing of God and wisdom. By claiming that this *logos* became flesh, John is taking a familiar idea of his culture and infusing it with new meaning—and for the time, a rather absurd meaning at that.

And it still is. If we toss about the idea of "God in the flesh" as if it were just that thing we believe, we are not tuned in to the shock and even offense that John's opening lines would have generated. Christianity is a weird religion, folks.

And just like the biblical notion of wisdom, this "Word become flesh" is not far off in the distance, but intimate with humans—accessible. Indeed, the whole purpose of the Word becoming flesh was to make humans *children of God* (John 1:12), or, as we read later in John's Gospel, to allow humans to experience the same mystical connection with the Father as the Son does (17:20–26).

The apostle Paul puts his own fine point on Jesus and wisdom: *He [God] is the source of your life in Christ Jesus, who became for us wisdom from God* (1 Cor. 1:30). Christ does not become wisdom for us by delivering a set of clearer ground rules for the game of life, but by peeling back the curtain to reveal the thicker existence of life with God: *God's mystery . . . is Christ himself, in whom are hidden all the treasures of wisdom and knowledge* (Col. 2:3).

Jesus, who is wisdom incarnate, gives us access to the Creator to reveal hidden things and invites us to seek out our sacred responsibility to perceive God's unscripted presence here and now.

Think About It: *Four* Gospels

This isn't quantum physics. There are four Gospels. But this is going somewhere.

The New Testament begins with four versions of the life of Jesus, and, as anyone can tell by reading them side by side, they don't exactly match up. They don't record the same events, and even when they do, the accounts sometimes differ rather significantly. That fact has been a cause of concern for some of the faithful, especially in modern times, when this disharmony has been used as evidence of their historical unreliability. After all, if the Gospels can't even agree on basic information at this key moment in the story, what good are they to tell us about the life of Jesus?!

Too often the response to this modern reaction has been to acknowledge that there are some differences, but they are minor and they don't really amount to much, blah, blah, blah. But a defensive, protective mindset misses a golden opportunity to see wisdom in action yet again.

Rather than defending the Gospels *against* their (self-evident) diversity, we should be asking ourselves why they are different at all. Why are there four versions of Jesus's life out there?

I can think of a few reasons why these differences exist. No one was taking notes as Jesus was talking, and so the stories got jumbled by the time they went from oral to written form. And we humans have faulty memories and "remember" events differently.

But I think the main reason they differ so much is this. Each Gospel writer took it upon himself to *shape*—not simply report—the story of Jesus the way he saw fit, to present Jesus not as an academic exercise in historical accuracy, but as a way of encouraging and strengthening the community for which he was writing.

To put it another way, each Gospel is its own unique *retelling* of the life of Jesus centered on the *needs of each writer's community of faith*. We're in wisdom territory here again, folks.

The Gospel writers weren't thinking, "Gee whillikers, I hope my story wins the accuracy contest and winds up making it into the Bible." They were more like pastors leading and encouraging everyday people to make sense of their lives as they walk the path of faith and trust in God. Each in its own way, the Gospels are answering the question, "How do you connect with the Savior here and now?"

Each Gospel is tailored for an audience, which means the Gospel writers were not simply focused on the life of Jesus, but—as wisdom demands—reading the situation.

John's Gospel, for example, is the maverick of the four. Most of what Jesus says and does here isn't found in the other three. There is no one simple answer for why this is so, but we can see that John was clearly crafting his story for his community.

John pits Jesus against "the Jews" rather than specifically the religious elite (scribes, lawyers), as the other three Gospels do. That has come across—understandably—as anti-Semitic and historically has been used to justify vilifying Jews (throughout much of German history at least as far back as Martin Luther and in Mel Gibson's *The Passion of the Christ*). But charging *John* with anti-Semitism doesn't cut it. The term is freighted in our day with a lot of history that isn't relevant for John's time. Many scholars have surmised that John's language actually gives us a window into the struggles of his community.

When John was written (probably somewhere in the 90s CE), there was no "Christianity" per se. Christianity as a distinct faith didn't really hit the ground until a bit later in the second century, when it emerged as a largely Gentile faith. But John was written when Jewish–Gentile division was just beginning, and Jewish believers especially might have been ostracized, thrown out of synagogues, and otherwise given a hard time. John's so-called anti-Jewish rhetoric was a commentary on his day.

In other words, John's phrasing was *an act of wisdom*: he was translating the Jesus story for his situation. It should therefore not be taken to be a timeless template for Jewish–Christian relations, but neither is it to be tossed aside as simply bigoted.

Supporting today John's rhetoric is not a sign of faithfulness to scripture, but a failure to accept the sacred responsibility of making the ancient text our own for our time. By aligning ourselves with John's rhetoric we would, ironically, not be following what John is actually doing—which is bringing the Jesus story to bear on the circumstances of his community's here and now. When we reproduce John's rhetoric today, after centuries of Jewish persecution and suffering, too often in the name of Christ, we are not reading *our* moment—and therefore not exercising wisdom.

One more example from the many in John's Gospel concerns the cleansing of the Temple. The other three Gospels place it at the beginning of Passion Week, Jesus's first act after he enters Jerusalem the week of his crucifixion. John, however, places the Temple cleansing at the beginning of Jesus's ministry, in chapter 2. I say "places," because John is certainly deliberately relocating this scene from the end to the beginning.

Historically speaking, Jesus didn't cleanse the Temple this early. Had he actually done so, his movement never would have gotten off the ground and John's Gospel wouldn't have gotten past chapter 3. Cleansing the Temple would have led to Jesus's arrest and crucifixion, as it does in the other Gospels. It would have been like a protest movement to reform American politics that began with the torching of the Capitol. The movement would have come to an abrupt halt.

But John's relocation of this episode isn't a "mistake." That's the vital point here. It is an intentional move on his part to paint his portrait of Jesus.

John is quite keen on establishing Jesus's divine authority right away, by both the signs Jesus performs (like turning water to wine, also in chapter 2) and the speeches Jesus gives. John's Jesus is certainly the most divine portrait of Jesus in the four Gospels. It is in John's Gospel that Jesus makes regular claims to his unique and intimate connection with God, much more so than in the other three, even appropriating the divine name "I AM" for himself.*

Similarly, John doesn't bother with a birth story (only Matthew and Luke do). John wants to establish Jesus's divine authority from the very beginning—he is the Word who was with God at creation and is God. John's birth story isn't so much missing as replaced with a story of Jesus's divine origin.

Likewise in chapter 1, Jesus appears at the Jordan River where John the Baptist (not the author of the Gospel!) is living up to his name—baptizing his fellow Jews to cleanse them of sin. Though Jesus is milling about in the story, he does not actually get baptized in John's Gospel, even though his baptism is quite prominent in the other Gospels. Jesus does some baptizing himself (which is not mentioned by the other three Gospels), but he himself is not baptized.

The reason John mutes Jesus's baptism is perhaps easy to see: John's divinely exalted and authoritative Jesus should not need to be forgiven of sins. The other Gospels handle this problem differently.

---

* See, for example, John 8:24. English translations often read *I am he* (as does the NRSV), but "I AM" is better. The phrase alludes to Exodus 3:14, where Moses asks for God's name, which God gives as *I am who I am*. "I AM" in Hebrew (*'hyh*) is thought to be the basis for the divine name Yahweh (*yhwh*).

They present the baptism as something like Jesus's royal coronation, in which he received public approval from God for his ministry. (Matthew, Mark, and Luke all include God's heavenly voice approving of Jesus, perhaps echoing Psalm 2:7, but John does not.)

That's enough of John. The other Gospels also have their own flavor.

Matthew's Gospel, for example, has by far the most citations of the Old Testament of any of the Gospels. He also seems to be intent on presenting Jesus as a new and improved Moses. In the Sermon on the Mount (chaps. 5–7), like Moses, Jesus is on a mountain delivering laws to the people below. In fact, as we saw earlier, Jesus places his authority above Moses's—his speech is punctuated by *You have heard that it was said [in the Law] . . . but I say to you . . .* In Luke, Jesus delivers a similar speech, but *on a level place* rather than on a mountain (6:17). Luke's portrait of Jesus is different than Matthew's.

Matthew's audience is largely Jewish—meaning Jewish followers of Jesus who would want to see that Jesus was deeply connected to Jewish tradition rather than overthrowing it (as some Gentile believers might have thought). Hence, Matthew's birth story of Jesus (which has virtually no overlap at all with Luke's, by the way) includes the scene of King Herod's massacre of infants (as an attempt to get at Jesus) and Jesus's flight to safety in Egypt.

This scene is probably less a piece of history than an intentional echo of the story of Moses: at his birth Moses escapes Pharaoh's edict to massacre male infants, and Moses later also fled from Pharaoh to save his own life. And both Moses and Jesus return home after being given the divine all-clear sign, and the wording is too similar to be accidental:

Get up, take the child and his mother, and go to the land of Israel, <u>for those who were seeking the child's life are dead.</u> (Matt. 2:20)

Go back to Egypt; <u>for all those who were seeking your life are dead.</u> (Exod. 4:19)

Only in Matthew does Jesus take a Moses-like trip.

Matthew, Mark, and Luke all include the lesson about new wine and old wineskins mentioned earlier, but they differ. Mark simply says that the new wine will burst the old wineskins (2:22). You're left with the impression that there isn't much use for old wine or old wineskins at all. Matthew adds a twist at the end. By putting new wine in new wineskins, *both* the new wine and the old wineskins are preserved (9:17). This way of putting it would make sense for a Jewish readership that might have been startled at Mark's more blunt words.

Luke goes in a very different and somewhat unexpected direction. After repeating the idea that new wine needs to go into new wineskins, Luke adds: *And no one after drinking old wine desires new wine, but says, "The old is good"* (5:36–39). This sounds backwards. Luke seems to be prioritizing Jewish tradition over Jesus—yes, the new wine belongs in new wineskins, but the old wine is better.

Luke's twist also has a purpose, though to be honest, I'm not really sure what that is. Since this lesson comes in the middle of a section in which Jesus is challenged by religious leaders (about fasting and keeping the sabbath), this twist may be a dig against them. Though the religious leaders claim to be the traditionalists and Jesus the dangerous innovator, Jesus is delivering a punchy retort that he is more aligned with the old ways than they are. They are the blundering innovators who actually cloud God's ways. I could be wrong, of course, but that makes most sense to me at the moment.

I'd rather stop now than go on for five hundred more pages talking about how the Gospel stories differ. My point here is simply this: each Gospel is a *deliberate* shaping of the life of Jesus to address the needs of the community.

According to the reigning theory, Mark was written first and was used as the basis for Matthew and Luke—and they *adjusted Mark's Gospel as they saw fit*, either by changing Mark to suit themselves or including scenes that Mark doesn't. We might call that dishonest, bad writing, plagiarism, or the like, but let's not impose our own rules onto ancient writers. The Gospel writers, rather, were adapting and shaping the relatively recent history of Jesus of Nazareth, even freely editing the work of others, in order to present Jesus meaningfully to their communities of faith.

But beyond the four Gospels, the New Testament as a whole is one big act of wisdom—its writers reimagine God in light of the present moment, in light of their faith in Jesus as God's Messiah. Their work ties Jesus to the past, but also takes the faith of old far beyond the pages of their sacred text, in more surprising—even startling—ways than we've seen thus far.

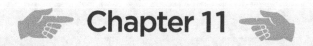

Chapter 11

Reimagining God the Jesus Way

Just Hear Me Out

Well, we're moving right along here at a pretty good clip; let's recap for a moment.

God is not a helicopter parent, and the Bible isn't set up to tell us what to do. God is a wise parent and the Bible is an ancient, often ambiguous, and undeniably diverse text, and as such invites us to accept our sacred responsibility of discerning the moment and of perceiving how God is present here and now. That is the life of wisdom, God's Plan A, which the Bible, by its very nature, points us toward.

We see already throughout the Bible how its various writers, living at different times and places and under different circumstances, found themselves needing to think of God differently—to reimagine God when older perceptions (which made sense earlier) could no longer account for their experience. And probably the biggest factors that affected the ancient Israelites were the crisis of exile and centuries of foreign rule that followed, especially Greek culture. How could they stay connected to the God of old when they were in such a different time and place and the God of old seemed so out of touch?

With Jesus, Israel's tradition was adjusted to account for this unexpected Messiah. We've looked at some of these adjustments already, but now we are going to zero in on other kinds of adjustments that

were more sweeping and controversial—where central Jewish ideas
and beliefs rooted in the Bible itself were reimagined.

Where new wine really needed new wineskins.

Which brings me (obviously) to the New York Yankees.

I don't mean to annoy anyone, but the New York Yankees are the
most successful sports franchise in the solar system (look it up). As
of summer 2018, they've played in more than one-third of all World
Series ever played (40 out of 113) and they won the World Series 27
times. No other sports franchise comes close, though it's cute when
they try.

I only bring this up to say that they were successful not by stub-
bornly sticking to tradition but by adjusting to changes in the game
over the last century. The game has changed in so many ways it's
hard to count, and I won't even try, for fear that those of you who
aren't interested in baseball might shut down—if you're, say, a
Communist or from Denmark and don't care for baseball, just substitute some worthless activity, like tennis or gardening. Just trust
me. It's changed. If you entered a time machine and brought back
players from the 1920s and 1930s, like Babe Ruth or Lou Gehrig,
and put them in today's starting lineup, they would be like lost
children.

You can never rest on past tradition. Success requires adapting
tradition to survive. That's the wise thing to do.

I'd like to thank the Yankees for helping me sum up a central
point of the book, but this brings me to a question that maybe some
of you have already been asking: "At what point do we cross the line
from *adapting* a tradition, so it can survive, to *compromising* the tradition beyond recognition?"

That is the big question, I think. And answering that question has been the struggle of Jewish and Christian theology since forever.

When Major League Baseball uniforms went from their traditional wool/wool blends to double-knit polyester in the early 1970s, the Yankees followed the trend. No biggie. The Yankee tradition is still intact. But what if they moved to Wyoming and called themselves the Cowpokes? Or changed their uniforms from home pinstripes and away gray to green, gold, and red? Then all hell—every square inch of it—would break loose.

Sometimes reading the New Testament feels like moving to Wyoming rather than switching to polyester uniforms.

I'm probably stretching the baseball analogy (and I don't care), but I'm doing my best to get across something about the New Testament that is so very crucial but also often misunderstood, if not ignored and resisted.

The Jesus movement owes its existence to a thousand and more years of Israelite and Jewish tradition. There is no wavering from that point among the New Testament writers, and any attempt to build a thick wall between the gospel and the Old Testament would be like saying the study of the space–time continuum owes nothing to Einstein.

But as great as Einstein was, his theories didn't anticipate quantum physics, the study of the weird world of very, very small atomic and subatomic particles. In fact, Einstein didn't know what to do with all of that (which is probably the only thing I have in common with Einstein).

The New Testament writers were quite often on a very different page from those in the long tradition that birthed the Jesus movement—not always, but often, and at crucial moments. Even if we take into account the diversity of that Jewish tradition, which we've seen within the Old Testament and in the Judaism that followed, still, the New Testament writers talk about Jesus in ways that the tradition didn't anticipate and that stretches the tradition to the breaking point.

The New Testament writers clearly respected and revered their deep Jewish tradition. But they were also clearly not bound to the script of that tradition, even on some points that had been non-negotiable. Explaining Jesus required new directions and new ways of thinking.

New wine can't be contained in old wineskins, and all that.

Paul Reimagines the God of Moses

It's no secret that the Law of Moses is a big deal in the Old Testament. It makes up most of the first five books, the Pentateuch (or Torah)—half of Exodus, all of Leviticus, and most of Numbers and Deuteronomy. These commands were given to Moses by God on Mt. Sinai, and they weren't presented to Israel as thoughts or suggestions to mull over, but laws, a contract, so to speak, the breaking of which would result in anything from a time-out or a cleansing ceremony to excommunication or even execution.

We've already seen that the Old Testament Law is surprisingly ambiguous and diverse—it's begging to be debated and deliberated over, which is exactly what we see happening in the Old Testament and also in some of Jesus's teachings. But once we get to the other parts of the New Testament, we sense a mood shift, with Paul especially. He keeps bringing the Law up—like he's trying to wrap his head around what place the Law has in light of this surprising story of Jesus, a crucified and risen Messiah.

Paul is notoriously hard to pin down, but let me try to sum up the gist of his thinking.

At times Paul argues that the Law is God's gift to Israel and even cites Torah as something to be obeyed. Other times—and more often—Paul affirms the Law as fine and good, though only as far as it goes. It really can't keep anyone on the straight and narrow. The Israelites had centuries to make it so, but their story is shot through with disobedience and ended in exile. The Law was "powerless" be-cause humanity (including Israel) was under the thumb of Sin and Death,* a story that has its roots back in the Garden of Eden with the disobedience of Adam and the punishment of death.

But what the Law couldn't do, Paul says, Jesus did. By his death and resurrection, Sin and Death are defeated, thus freeing us to be obedient to the Law of God, which Paul sums up as loving others in a spirit of humility in imitation of Jesus.

But, judging from Paul's words, some Jewish believers didn't see it that way. They were arguing that Gentile followers of Jesus weren't really full-fledged members until they demonstrated their obedience to Mosaic Law (especially that Gentile males had to be circumcised just as Jews were). Paul responded that the Torah, which held such a central place in Judaism, has now moved to the side. Now Jesus occupied that central place. Otherwise, Jesus's self-sacrifice on our behalf—the act of God's pure grace—means nothing.

---

* I capitalize these words because Paul almost seems to give them a personality, namely, in Romans 5:12–21.

Paul even goes so far as to say that the main purpose of the Law was to show just how bad we are at keeping it (the Law *multiplied* the trespass, as he puts it in Rom. 5:20) and to show, therefore, how great God's grace is by comparison. And in Galatians, where Paul is particularly irked, he makes the rather surprising argument that the Law given on Mt. Sinai is symbolically represented—and let this sink in—by the Egyptian slave woman Hagar. Freedom *from* the Law is represented by Hagar's mistress, Abraham's wife, Sarah (4:21–26).

So Sarah—mind you, the wife of Abraham, the father of Israel— represents freedom *from* the Law. We can see why Paul had a lot of opposition from Jewish believers.

Paul's thinking is complicated, and what he says about the Law predictably fills floors of libraries, keeps young doctoral students busy and paranoid, and can get you pummeled in the dark back allies of academia. But still, you can't help but read Paul and walk away with the sense that he's not fully with the ancient program where Torah is central to knowing God's purposes.

You don't find Paul's line of thinking reflected in the Old Testament or in the various paths of Judaism after the exile. Just look at all 176 verses of Psalm 119, the longest psalm in the Old Testament. God is praised over and over again for this wonderful gift of Torah:

> *Do not take the word of truth [the Law] utterly out of my*
> *   mouth,*
> *for my hope is in your ordinances.* (verse 43)

> *My soul languishes for your salvation;*
> *I hope in your word [Law].* (verse 81)

Oh, how I love your law!
It is my meditation all day long. (verse 97)

Your word [Law] is a lamp to my feet
and a light to my path. (verse 105)

I just can't see Paul saying any of those things, and he doesn't. Or better, all the praise Jewish tradition gives to the Law Paul gives to Christ, who is *the end of the law* (Rom. 10:4)—meaning not the rejection of Law as such, but the end goal that the Law was driving toward all along.

Paul doesn't reject the Law of Moses, as some in Christian history have thought, but he does marginalize it, decenter it, by placing at the center of God's plan for the world not *our* obedience to Torah, but *Christ's* obedience to go through with the crucifixion to defeat Sin and God's raising of Jesus from the dead to defeat Death.

Am I missing something, or is this a major shift, folks?* You don't get to Paul's gospel simply from reading the Old Testament. You need to be convinced, first, that Jesus is the way, and then *reimagine God and the faith of old to account for it*, which is to say, to read the moment—the Jesus moment—and adjust the tradition in light of it.

That's the message Paul delivered, and judging from his letters he got a lot of resistance.

Again, let's not be surprised about that. In a way, it's easy for Christians today to say that the poor blokes just didn't get it. But in

---

* Rhetorical question.

another way, we need to understand why. Paul was expecting a lot—a rethinking of the heart of the tradition, the role of Torah.

Going Off Script

The whole matter comes to a head with two specific laws that keep coming up in Paul's letters: circumcision and not eating unclean food.

God commanded that Abraham circumcise himself, his son Isaac, and any other males of his household and that circumcising males on the eighth day from then on would be an *everlasting covenant*, which sounds serious, because it is (see Gen. 17). Failure to keep the command would mean being cut off from the people, which probably means something like excommunication, but in any case is one of the more delightful puns you will read anywhere. The laws about clean and unclean animals are given in Leviticus 11 and Deuteronomy 14, commands from God to Moses on Mt. Sinai, and are no more negotiable than any other commands.

These two laws in particular were central to Jewish identity in Paul's day. They had become social badges of honor to distinguish Jews from Gentiles, something concrete to hang on to amid the persistent religious chaos introduced by centuries of Greek and Roman ways. That's why I wear my Yankees jersey in Phillies country. I do it, at great risk to myself, to let the world—the world, mind you—know that I am different. I belong to another tribe. I am special.

Paul argued tirelessly that these badges of honor, which he often refers to as *works of the law* (for example, Gal. 2:16), are not what identify people as children of God. They may have at one time, and they served their purpose. But now faith in Jesus and love of others are the badges of honor.

That's a pretty radical move for a Jew to make. And yet Paul's creative take on the Law isn't all that different from the kind of Jewish reflection on Torah we've been looking at. Though going off in a very unexpected direction, Paul's creative handling of the Law is a classic Jewish interpretive move. He is exercising wisdom.

Paul is reinterpreting the purpose of Torah, because times have changed—Jesus has come. Now Paul has to account for something not accounted for by Israel's tradition: a crucified and risen Messiah. Even though his fellow Jews probably wouldn't have found any fault in principle with rethinking Torah, for many Paul's reimagining of God went too far.

They weren't willing to move to Wyoming.*

Paul didn't wake up one morning with radical thoughts about the Law out of nowhere. He was awakened to the Spirit of Christ and the conviction that Jesus, because he defeated death, had something for both Gentiles and Jews, with neither being superior to the other. This has proved to be nothing short of an evolutionary innovation in the Jewish tradition, and without it Christianity, which began its life as a Jewish sect, would not have become an essentially Gentile phenomenon already by the second century CE.

But—if I may editorialize—where Paul might have pushed too far is how he argued his point from scripture. Paul made the case that

---

* "Why does he keep bringing up baseball . . . and Yankee baseball?" (Spoken in your best Jim Gaffigan voice.)

Jesus's replacing Torah as the center of the tradition and the full and equal inclusion of the Gentiles were part of God's plan *all along*—going back to the days of Abraham himself.

Consider Abraham, Paul tells us. He was a friend of God, was he not, long before Moses and the Law? Hence, the Law was never really necessary to God's plan, only faith was—the faith that Abraham had when he *believed* (better, *trusted*) in God (Gen. 15:6). The Law came much later and its role, rather, was (as I mentioned above) to expose the depth of sin, or, as he puts it in Galatians 4:1–7, to act as temporary trustee for God's people until Jesus came. Then the Law could step aside and we could be released from the Law's Hagarlike bondage.

Paul's take that the Abraham story marginalizes the Law feels forced, especially since very soon after Genesis 15 Abraham is required to obey God, *so that* the promises can be fulfilled. For example: *I have chosen him [Abraham], that he may charge his children and his household after him to keep the way of the LORD by doing righteousness and justice;* **so that** *the LORD may bring about for Abraham what he has promised him* (Gen. 18:19). I would love to have been a fly on the wall for how Jewish believers might have responded to Paul's take on the Abraham story.

Or look at Romans 9:22–29, where Paul engages in a bit of biblical interpretation that is, frankly, tortured. He strings together several passages from the prophets Hosea and Isaiah that speak of God mercifully calling those who are *not my people* and *not beloved* back to the fold. Who are these "not" people? In Hosea and Isaiah they are rebellious Israelites who are restored as God's people. Paul, however, reads *not my people* and *not beloved* as referring to Gentiles, which is a conclusion one can only arrive at either by simply not paying attention—or by *reimagining Israel's story creatively* because the circumstances demand it.

I don't read these Old Testament passages the way Paul does, but then again my context is different. I don't feel the need to tie the Jesus story to Israel's tradition like this. Maybe I should, I don't know. But I don't. This does show, however, how determined Paul was to somehow tie his experience—the unexpected influx of Gentiles who were following Jesus as savior—to Israel's tradition. The question it raises, though, is whether in doing so Paul is actually pouring new wine into old wineskins—trying too hard to make Jesus fit the old ways.

But that's an in-house debate. And I could be wrong, and I'm sure God is willing to let it slide if I am. I'm just trying to follow the twists and turns of the Bible. Either way the point stands: the gospel forced Paul to go back and reconsider Israel's story from a point of view that the story itself wasn't set up to handle. And not just any old part of the story, but the heart of it, the Law of Moses.

Other New Testament writers also make Jesus-centered radical moves that touch at the core of Jewish tradition.

1 Temple Avenue, Back Room, Jerusalem

We might say today that God is everywhere at once, but that is not how the ancient Israelites (or any other ancient people) thought. True, on the one hand, God's throne is in heaven, the earth is his footstool, and no structure can contain him (Isa. 66:1). On the other hand, God does most certainly have a residence, and the Old Testament makes quite a big deal of it.

At first, it was the Tabernacle—a tent, a moveable house of worship—that Moses and the Israelites built in the wilderness after the exodus. This worship tent is such an important structure that Exodus 25–40, the last sixteen chapters of the book, is mostly taken up with describing how exactly it was built according to a heavenly blueprint. After the Israelites settled in the land of Canaan and the monarchy was established by David, the honor of building the permanent structure, the Temple, went to David's son Solomon (1 Kings 6).

The Temple was an elaborate structure—perhaps too elaborate—with all its gold, silver, bronze, and precious wood. But despite all of that, the Temple represented God's presence with the Israelites. It was where sacrifices were made and where God appeared to the high priest once a year on the Day of Atonement (Yom Kippur) in the inner space called the Holy of Holies, a fifteen-foot square back room that housed the holy ark of the covenant, which contained, among other things, a copy of the Ten Commandments, the symbol of Yahweh's tie to his people. The failure to maintain the proper worship of God in the Temple led directly to the razing of the Temple and the deportation of the residents of Jerusalem in 586 BCE.

The Temple was, to say the least, a big deal for Israelite religion, so much so that the first order of business upon returning to the land in 538 BCE was to rebuild it. Completed around 516 BCE and though merely a shadow of its former glory, it was nevertheless proof that Yahweh had returned to be with his people. This Second Temple, as it is called, received a major face-lift around 19 BCE during the days of Roman rule under King Herod the Great and remained the central symbol of Judaism until the Romans razed it in 70 CE, a too familiar replay of the Babylonian invasion centuries before.

The Temple was still standing during Jesus's and Paul's lifetimes. On the one hand, its presence was simply a given—the central symbol of Jewish identity and God's presence. On the other, the Temple simply isn't a focal point in the New Testament. It's not a treasured part of the plan—which is truly strange if we remember that the Jesus movement was fundamentally Jewish.

We're coming to another major reimagining of God in the New Testament.

We will recall that Jesus famously cleansed the Temple by overturning the tables of the money changers. Jesus was angry, and that's fine. The Temple was sacred and not supposed to feel like you're at a tailgating party. And yet, we might wonder what animals and money changers were doing there in the first place. The animals were for sacrifice, and the money changers allowed Jewish pilgrims, who came from all over, to exchange their pagan money (with the image of Caesar on the coins) for shekels, so they could buy animals to sacrifice (rather than schlepping them from who knows where).

Jesus isn't just venting. The act is deeply symbolic, especially in John's version of this episode (2:13–25): the Temple has outgrown its usefulness. With no money changers, there is no sacrifice; with no sacrifice, well, Judaism would need to figure something out. And as you read that, again, remember that *Jesus and the early followers of Jesus were Jewish* and not angling to start a new religion.

We are at a pivotal moment in understanding the significance of Jesus: the ancient story of Israel and Israel's God was hinting at an upheaval, a shift in direction.

When asked by the Jewish authorities to give them some indication that he had the right to turn over tables, Jesus answered (and this is only in John, who you remember is very big on establishing Jesus's authority), *Destroy this temple, and in three days I will raise it up* (2:19). They all thought Jesus might be a bit bonkers in the brain, since Herod's renovations were still going on forty-six years later. But John goes on to explain that Jesus was talking about his body—that he would be crucified and raised on the third day.

Jesus *is* the Temple. Talk about an upheaval.

Money changers and animals are no longer needed. Neither is the Temple. The Romans would destroy the Temple in 70 CE, never to be rebuilt. But Jesus will still be here.

It might help to remember that John is writing all this about two decades after the Temple fell. John is taking the time to explain how the destruction of the Temple speaks to the significance of Jesus. The other three Gospels were written much closer to 70 CE (Mark perhaps a bit before). They don't include this exchange that John has—perhaps because they hadn't yet had time to process how the cataclysmic fall of the holy sanctuary fit with the gospel.

A new era of "God's residence" was dawning, already hinted at in John 1:14: *The Word became flesh and lived among us, and we have seen his glory.* The Greek word behind *lived* is better rendered *tented* or *tabernacled*—it is the same word used in the Greek translation of the Old Testament for Moses's Tabernacle in the wilderness. John says that, as the glory of Yahweh filled the Tabernacle in the Old Testament (Exod. 40:34), we see Jesus's glory as he "tabernacled" with us.

All of which is to say we are witnessing here a rather seismic shift in how God's presence is perceived, one that goes beyond anything the tradition had made room for. And we can see why some accused Jesus of blasphemy.

But Jesus *is* here. Things *are* different. The *idea* of God's presence remains as it did in former days—that is the "old treasure." But the new treasure—the new wine that the old wineskin of the Temple can't contain—is *how* God's presence is now experienced: through Jesus.

Paul, as he tends to, takes this a step farther. The Spirit of God now dwells in all believers, so that Paul can refer to the church at Corinth as a whole as *God's temple* (1 Cor. 3:16) and each person's body also as *a temple of the Holy Spirit* (6:19). And in the final book of the New Testament, Revelation, the end goal of the people of God is to dwell with God intimately and directly, without any need for a temple (21:22).

For the Jesus movement, the Temple's ultimate usefulness was in foreshadowing the presence of God in Jesus and his followers. This was not where the story of Israel was supposed to go. Ezekiel, besides talking about sour grapes, had a vision of the glory of the future Temple that spans nine chapters (40–48). It is rather detailed, as you can imagine, but the punch line is that this Temple will be quite a sight, truly fitting for God's glory. As God says, *This is the place of my throne and the place for the soles of my feet, where I will reside among the people of Israel forever* (43:7).

The reimagining of God in light of the gospel has no need of this structure. The plan has changed.

Christians today might take this sort of thing for granted. Temples are not part of our experience, but in the first century the Temple was a thousand-year-old symbol of God's actual presence.

Nothing could really approximate for us today this first-century upheaval—perhaps removing any and all Christian symbols from our houses of worship: stained glass, crosses, crucifixes, bells, organs, icons, altars, pulpits, and lecterns. We might say, "That's okay. We'll miss them, but we still have Jesus." And that's the point, really. What a very Christian thing to say. Christians have never had a Temple in Jerusalem where God's glory dwelt.

Let's not lose the big picture here. The really central point in all this is that the biblically rooted tradition of a holy sanctuary for God shifts from a structure to a person—and then that person's followers. That sort of thinking only came about because the circumstances demanded it. Jesus inspired a major midcourse change in direction.

What eventually became "Christianity" began as a Jewish sect—a sect that stretched the boundaries of Judaism to its limit. Eventually, like Jesus's wineskins, it stretched those boundaries too far.

And speaking of boundaries . . .

This Land Is My Land

You're probably sick of hearing it, but this is my book and I'll say it again for good measure: the Babylonian exile was a huge moment for the ancient Israelites, for several reasons, not the least of which was the loss of land and what that loss represented.

I know, I'm repeating myself. I do that a lot. My family is sick of it. We've already touched on all these points. But anytime you talk about the story of Israel in the Old Testament, you can't avoid saying "exile" about every third sentence. It was *the* great defeat, the crisis that threatened to bring an end to the faith of Abraham, but then wound up being the creative spark that paved the way for the un-broken existence of Judaism to this day, not to mention Christianity.

Exile drove Jews to think creatively about their past, face their present, and cast visions for the future.

Along with the Law and the Temple, land was central to Israel's story. We see it already at the beginning of the story with Abraham in Genesis 12. The first thing God does after calling Abraham is give him a tour of some prime real estate, the land of Canaan, that will eventually go to Abraham's descendants. That is Yahweh's promise to this chosen man and the nation that will come from him.

The stories of the Pentateuch, Genesis through Deuteronomy, are not stand-alone lessons of some sort. They are more like an entrance ramp to the promised land—the Israelites grow from a single family, to an extended family, to tribes; after a period of slavery in Egypt, they finally emerge as a nation ready to take possession of the land to fulfill the promise to father Abraham.

Now the real drama can begin.

The land was a gift of God, but with a condition. The people would keep the land as long as they obeyed Yahweh—we're not talking perfection here, but worshiping Yahweh exclusively and without all the accoutrements of the surrounding pagan nations, like idols.

The monarchy was to have brought a central organization to the Israelites to ensure not only their safety from enemies (though that), but also their fidelity to God's Law. Unfortunately—and to make a long story short—the monarchy was a disaster largely because the kings really blew it.

David's reign seemed to be going well—for exactly six chapters (2 Sam. 5–10). In chapter 11, David forced Bathsheba to have sex with him and arranged for her husband, Uriah, to be conveniently killed in battle to cover up her pregnancy. From then on, David's reign was marked by one disaster or disappointment after another until his death.

His son Solomon wasn't much better. Sure, under his rule, Israel's borders extended as far as they ever did, and he established a real kingdom with a bureaucracy, standing army, and so on (1 Kings 4). His wisdom was legendary (and probably exaggerated), but the good times were short lived. He amassed a lot of wealth and horses, not to mention foreign wives—things Deuteronomy warns kings not to do (17:16–17). Then, after spending seven years building an elaborate Temple, he spent almost twice as long (thirteen years) building an even more elaborate palace for himself with so much gold that the writer of 1 Kings feels the need to keep bringing it up. And silver? Fuhgedaboudit. That became as common as stones (10:27).

Bottom line, we're talking about an opulent existence worthy of its own cable reality series. But at the end, what marked the demise of the united monarchy was Solomon's foreign wives, who seduced him into setting up worship centers in the land for their foreign gods (1 Kings 11). That and Solomon's history of using forced labor, especially from the northern tribes (David and Solomon were from Judah in the south), and before you know it the country breaks along the north–south fault line and two nations are formed around 930 BCE: Israel in the north and Judah in the south.

So far not a complete disaster. At least after all this they still have their land.

But the clock is ticking. By 722, Samaria, the capital of the larger nation of Israel is conquered by the Assyrians, and the southern nation falls to the Babylonians 136 years later.

The unthinkable happened. Most of Israelite territory is run by (gulp) the Assyrians. Israel is no longer a people of the land promised to Abraham. A rump state, Judah, is left in the south. And how would you feel if America were conquered and all that remained was Alabama to represent what once was? You can see my point.

Land is a major—one might even say *the* major—running theme of the entire Old Testament. Most of its thirty-nine books deal with gaining it, maintaining it, losing it anyway, and then returning to it—specifically we're talking about twenty-eight of the thirty-nine books: Joshua through Nehemiah (eleven) and all the major and minor prophets (seventeen).

It is not an exaggeration to say that the backdrop of the entire Old Testament drama is about how keeping or losing the land is dependent on Israel's religious obedience.

The Judahites returned to the land in 538 BCE, a testament to God's faithful promise keeping. Surely now all will get back to normal. But their return was not truly complete until they had their own king sitting on the throne in Jerusalem, which basically never happened. Centuries pass waiting out first the Persians and then the Greeks, and the hope was kept alive, at least for some. One day, a king will rise in the line of David and thus restore the fortunes of his people, and the land will be theirs again. That was the "messianic hope" for many.

Enter Jesus.

In the midst of such a drama rooted in an ancient and irrevocable promise of God, Jesus reimagines a God who has no interest in maintaining national borders—God is no longer interested in his own promise that goes back to the days of Abraham.

Judging from the Sermon on the Mount, for example (Matt. 5–7),

Jesus has no place for nationalism or political power, whether Roman or Jewish. Recovering the land of Israel—meaning an Israel the Jews run as their own with their own king, as in the old days—never gets so much as a whisper of support in the Gospels or anywhere else in the New Testament. Rather, the opposite is the norm.

Jesus was on trial and accused of claiming to be "King of the Jews," which was treason against Rome, since Caesar already had someone filling that position at the moment—namely, Pontius Pilate. When interrogated by Pilate about his insurrection, Jesus famously replied: *My kingdom is not from this world. If my kingdom were from this world, my followers would be fighting to keep me from being handed over to the Jews. But as it is, my kingdom is not from here* (John 18:36).

So much for reestablishing the monarchy. What had been the whole point has now become no big deal. A central theme—if not *the* central theme—of Israel's long history is not even worthy of debate. Jerusalem will no longer play the central role in God's grand scheme.

Law, Temple, land. It's hard to find three more central elements of Israel's story. And all three experience a dramatic upheaval with the coming of Christ. Israel's storyline with its expected trajectory has been ruthlessly edited and taken in a new direction.

The circumstances demand it. The story has to be adjusted. God is reimagined. And the Bible already has a long history of doing just that.

Children of Abraham

As much as the early followers of Jesus reimagined Law, Temple, and land, there is another act of reimaging God that lies behind all three.

It is *the* issue that would come to give the Christian faith its shape in the centuries to come; an act of reimagination so daring even key figures of the New Testament couldn't see eye to eye about it.

The issue is what place Gentiles would have in this movement—specifically, whether Gentiles needed to adopt Jewish customs and practices in order to be considered true and full members of this Jesus movement, on equal standing with Jewish believers. At the very dawn of the Jesus movement, decisions had to me made about how closely this movement would be bound by biblical tradition. Once the gospel spread to the larger Greek speaking world, outside of Judea, the issue was bound to come up.

Those who felt strongly that Gentiles had to convert to Judaism had history—and common sense—on their side. The Law of Moses wasn't a pick-and-choose proposition, and although Gentile converts in the Old Testament are hard to find, we can presume that if any had wanted to be fully identified with the faith of Abraham, they would have needed to fall in line—especially with the command given to Abraham to circumcise *every* male of his household, which included his servants.

Also, in the book of Judith (Apocrypha), we have the example of the Ammonite Achior, who (in a fictitious account) helped the Israelites defeat the Assyrians, and later converted: *When Achior saw all that the God of Israel had done, he believed firmly in God. So he was circumcised, and joined the house of Israel, remaining so to this day* (Judith 14:10).

My point is simply that expecting Gentiles to observe the ancient customs of Judaism is hardly unreasonable. But this Jesus movement went in another direction, as we already saw briefly earlier with what Paul said about circumcision and dietary laws—Gentiles would not be bound to Jewish customs as an entrance point to being full-fledged members of the Jesus movement. They could, presumably, decide to accept some practices and not others, but Paul argues that they were not *bound* to do so, nor should anyone presume to hold a higher status in the movement by binding themselves to them.

Of course, Christianity has gone with Paul on the Gentile question, but that was not always the case. We read in Galatians 2 that Paul didn't see eye to eye on this with Peter, the head disciple, and James, Jesus's own brother. Actually, Paul thought everyone was on the same page regarding the Gentiles, but, as Paul put it, Peter and James seemed to have caved in to the pressure of "Judaizers"—Paul's not-so-subtle description of believers who wanted to hold fast to the traditions.

And in his own letter, James seems to have Paul—or at least Paul's ideas—in his sights:

> *What good is it, my brothers and sisters, if you say you have faith but do not have works? Can faith save you? If a brother or sister is naked and lacks daily food, and one of you says to them, "Go in peace; keep warm and eat your fill," and yet you do not supply their bodily needs, what is the good of that? So **faith by itself, if it has no works, is dead.***
>
> *But someone will say, "You have faith and I have works." **Show me your faith apart from your works, and I by my works will show you my faith**. You believe that God is one; you do well. Even the demons believe—and shudder. Do you want to be shown, you senseless person, that **faith apart from works is barren**? Was not **our ancestor Abraham** justified*

*by works when he offered his son Isaac on the altar? You see that
faith was active along with his works, and **faith was brought
to completion by the works**. Thus the scripture was fulfilled
that says, "Abraham believed God, and it was reckoned to him
as righteousness," and he was called the friend of God. You see
that **a person is justified by works and not by faith alone**.*
(James 2:14–24)

Paul's message was that we are justified by faith, not works. James
sees it differently. And both prove their case by appealing to the story
of Abraham!

The controversy that gripped the early years is hardly an issue now.
I don't know too many Christians today who avoid pork or lobster.
But what we take for granted now was at the beginning a massive and
controversial act of reimagination about who can rightly claim to be
the children of Abraham.

It wasn't clear what to do, and people disagreed—including some
key New Testament characters. Even then, reimagining God wasn't
easy or straightforward. Do we think it would be anything else for
us today?

* * *

God is one step ahead of us, it seems—always another surprise
around the corner that forces us to stand back and wonder what God
is up to and how to respond.

The belief that, in Jesus, God was making a grand and climactic
appearance on the world stage drove the earliest followers of Jesus
to reimagine God and what God was up to in the world—their

experience, their time and place, drove them to change their thinking, even about such important things as Law, Temple, land, and whether Israel's ancient traditions are binding on Gentiles.

But we can't really leave this topic without touching on something that is both central to the Christian faith and represents about as profound a reimagining of God in the story as we can imagine.

I'm talking about Easter—Jesus's crucifixion and resurrection. You know, those things that make Christianity what it is.

Chapter 12

Dying and Rising for Others

What Is God Up To?

Jesus, raised from the dead. Seems to be a pretty important idea in the New Testament. I think it's fair to say that it is *the* idea around which the entire gospel story revolves, though I suppose, like most things, that is up for debate. But here's a question worth asking: "Why resurrection at all?"

Why did God raise Jesus from the dead? What's the point? Was God just showing off? ("Look what I can do!") Why do *this*?

In my experience, that question isn't asked very often—sort of like, "Why is there coffee?" But it was certainly a question that the New Testament writers *had* to deal with—and they reimagined God in the process.

I can think of some reasons why the gospel includes resurrection, and they are all tied to Israel's story in some sense while at the same time (here we go again) moving beyond anything the Old Testament writers had in mind.

Resurrection from the dead is a metaphor in the Old Testament for returning from the Babylonian exile. In Ezekiel 37, mentioned earlier, the metaphorical dead bones of the exiled Jews are brought back to life. Babylon, after all, is the "death place," while the promised land is "life." Deuteronomy 30:15–20 doesn't talk about dry bones, but it gets at the same point: living in the land is "life" and being driven from the land is "death."

Hence—and I think we'll all appreciate the logic—if leaving the land is to die, then returning to the land is to come back to life, or "to rise from the dead."

I think this is one reason that all four Gospels tie the ministry of Jesus so closely to Israel's return from exile. They all introduce Jesus's ministry by citing (with differences, of course) the opening verses of a core return-from-exile passage in the Old Testament, Isaiah 40: *The voice of one crying out in the wilderness: "Prepare the way of the Lord, make his paths straight"* (Matt. 3:3; Mark 1:3; Luke 3:4; John 1:23).

Since this passage is cited by all four Gospels as a way of introducing Jesus's ministry, it looks as though the Gospel writers are all trying to say that Jesus's ministry will have something to do with bringing an end to the exile—of raising the nation back to life.

This would be accomplished by the Messiah ("anointed one")—a king in the line of David—taking his rightful place on the ancient throne in Jerusalem and thus reestablishing Israel's ancient monarchy. At least this is how Mary, the mother of Jesus, and Zechariah, the father of John the Baptist, see it. God has brought to Israel a mighty savior in the line of David, who will bring down the proud (Rome) and rescue Israel from all its enemies and haters (Luke 1:51–53, 69–73).

This was how at least some Jews thought about God's future deliverance, and all four Gospels are on board with it—the king is here, the exile is about to end. But as we continue reading the Gospels, ending the exile by being crowned king in Jerusalem is about the last thing on Jesus's mind. And the resurrection at the end of the story isn't the reconstituted nation's, but Jesus's and the establishment of the kingdom of heaven on earth.

Let's call that a rather significant shift in domestic and foreign policy.

Furthermore, rising from the dead, which is barely hinted at in the Old Testament, comes into its own during the Greek period—I'm thinking here about 2 Maccabees 7, which we've looked at. God will show his commitment, faithfulness, and justice to his people by raising them from the dead at the end of the age, so they too can take part in the kingdom of God.

To be raised from the dead as a reward for faithfulness to God and the Law was a given for many Jews (though not for the Sadducees, who thought that idea was rather ridiculous). But the Christian claim that Paul never tires of making, that "God raised Jesus from the dead," is a major twist in the plot—in fact, it was off script altogether.

God raising the dead wasn't a remarkable idea at the time. But God raising *one person* from the dead, as something that *already happened*—well, that's a head-scratcher.

The massive end-time resurrection has now become the resurrection of one man in the present time. And this is where it gets really confusing for readers of Paul (as if we needed more confusion about Paul's letters). Paul came to the conclusion that God's raising of Jesus is Phase 1 of the "end times." Phase 2 will come at some future time when all will be raised in the normal Jewish way of thinking about it. But (more confusion coming) the final judgment that God would announce at the future time (Judgment Day, we often call it) has, for Paul, already been announced for believers in Jesus now.

I know. Hang with me.

When Paul says to the church in Rome, for example, that they are *now justified by his [God's] grace* (Rom. 3:24), the earth-shattering part of that claim isn't *justified* or even *grace*, but the word *now*. It has already happened for believers in Jesus. The future is brought into the present time through Jesus.

Think of the resurrection as God unexpectedly going off script and bringing into the present time a bit of the future.

Jesus has experienced already (physical resurrection) what others will experience later at the "end." But for now, all those who are *in Christ* (Paul's rather mystical way of talking about the deep tie between Christ and believers; for example, Rom. 8:1; 2 Cor. 1:21) *already take part* in the future reality through being *united* with Jesus (as Paul puts it in Rom. 6:5). And so we read that believers *have been* raised from the dead, *have been* justified, and even *have been* seated with Christ in the heavenly places, not literally, but spiritually (Eph. 2:4–6).

To sum up, all that future stuff of Jewish theology is already a present spiritual reality for believers in Jesus, because Jesus has delivered a piece of that future to our front door.

It's okay to take some time to wrap our heads around all this. My point here isn't to get into all the nuances in the convoluted sentences of Paul's writings and figure it all out. My point is that Paul is thinking about resurrection (and God's judgment) in ways that simply aren't part of the Old Testament mindset or Jewish tradition up to this point.

Explaining Jesus's resurrection required an act of reimagining God to keep up with this unexpected move. Paul and other New Testament writers had to tie it to Israel's story somehow rather than dismissing it. Reading Paul's letters is like having a front row seat to watch the wheels turning in his head, for example, in Romans 5:12–21.

Israel's entire story both in the Old Testament and after the exile turns on the idea that obedience to God's Law brings life and blessing. Disobedience brings death and a curse. The solution to that problem brought on by disobedience is, understandably, to be more deeply committed to obeying the Law.

But if a crucified and raised Messiah is how God finally shows up—if that is God's unexpected "solution"—it makes you wonder, "What is the problem God is solving this way?"

Paul is about to turn the Jewish storyline inside out and upside down.

Failure to keep Torah, Paul argues, is not really *the* problem. If it were, the solution would have centered somehow on keeping Torah better. But since God's solution was to defeat death, maybe the deeper problem that God is interested in solving is death?

And death, after all, is something all humans share. And so defeating death is not God's response to the *Jewish* failure to keep the *Law*. It is a response to the universal fact of death, which is the story of all humanity, Jew and Gentile alike, rooted in the story of Adam and the forbidden fruit, long before Moses and the Law ever appeared on the scene.

Paul essentially responds to Israel's *main storyline* by saying, "All that was just prelude to what God is really up to—reversing the curse of death for everyone."

No one would arrive at a conclusion like that simply from reading the Old Testament. Rather, you have to start with seeing Jesus as the "solution," read the Bible backwards, so to speak, and reimagine God to account for this surprising turn of events.

The central event of the Christian faith, the resurrection of the Messiah and the defeat of death, isn't part of the Old Testament trajectory. To see God doing such a thing is to radically reimagine what kind of a God we are dealing with.

No, Seriously, What Is God Up To?

"Jesus died on the cross for you." Sort of rolls off the Christian tongue like rain off a metal roof. But here too we are looking at a significant act of reimagining the God of the Bible.

God raising the Messiah from the dead was enough to think about. But why did he have to die the way he did? It's not enough to say, "So he could rise from the dead." Jesus could have died any which way, at an old age, of some disease people got back then, trampled under a chariot by accident. But why a bloody and beaten mess on a Roman cross, a symbol of torture, intimidation, humiliation, and the unquestioned authority of the empire?

Perhaps Jesus had to die in this ritualistic and bloody way to be a sacrifice for our sins—which plays off the very prominent Old Testament idea of blood sacrifice. Paul uses Old Testament sacrificial language to describe the crucifixion, such as God's offering Jesus as a *sacrifice of atonement by his blood* (Rom. 3:25).

Seeing the crucifixion as a kind of sacrifice makes sense and it is certainly part of the New Testament vocabulary—though that raises the uncomfortable possibility that we are dealing with a human sacrifice to God, which is about as big a no-no in the Old Testament as anything. In Jeremiah 7:30–34, child sacrifice is what tipped the scales and led God to send the Babylonians as punishment.

In the Old Testament the tribe of Levi is a kind of "sacrifice" (Num. 3:12–13, 40–46). God claims repeatedly that the firstborn of the flock "belongs" to him. And this goes for *every* firstborn—humans too (see Exod. 13:2; 22:29). But God specifies that the Levites can serve as substitutes for all the firstborn. Instead of receiving a tribal allotment of land, the Levites will be God's own by serving as priests in the sanctuary. Elsewhere, animal sacrifice is the substitute for the firstborn, as in Exodus 13:13–15.

But there is no room for literally sacrificing a human, child or not, to atone for the sins of others, which is what we are dealing with in the crucifixion.

So the question is still out there: How can the blood of one sacrificed *person* atone for other people's sins? For that, we need to look elsewhere, starting with the prophet Isaiah.

Isaiah 52:13–53:12 speaks of a "suffering servant." This servant is in rough shape. He is so beaten he doesn't even look human. He is a man of suffering who, we read, *has borne **our** infirmities and carried **our** diseases, . . . was wounded for **our** transgressions, crushed for **our** iniquities* (53:4–5).

Many Christians are familiar with this portion of Isaiah, because it sounds so much like Jesus. In fact, who *else* could it be? No one else in the Bible suffers *for us*. It must be Jesus.

Well, I get it, but not so fast. Elsewhere in Isaiah, the servant is identified as Israel (41:8–9; 44:1–2, 21; 45:4; 48:20; 49:3; though in 63:11 he is Moses). The servant is certainly not some mystery person in the far distant future, but Israel here and now.

In Isaiah 52 and 53, then, this suffering servant is not a person, but Israel—specifically, those Judahites exiled to Babylon. The fact that the servant is referred to as "he" doesn't mean that Isaiah's suffering servant is one person. The language is poetic, as when God calls Israel his *wife* (as in Hos. 2:16–20). The suffering servant refers to those who actually suffered for all the other Judahites who were left behind in the land. *Their* return from exile meant healing and forgiveness for all.

Some suffered, and others benefitted.

This idea gets more explicit in 4 Maccabees, another Greek-era book of the Apocrypha. Toward the end, the author talks about the tyrant king Antiochus IV Epiphanes and those whom he martyred. These, the author says, are special—they have been consecrated and honored for giving their lives on behalf of the nation, allowing the homeland to be *purified* (from Antiochus's desecrations of the Temple mentioned earlier). The author sums it up this way:

> *These, then, who have been consecrated for the sake of God . . .*
> *having become, as it were, a **ransom for the sin of our nation**.*
> *And through the blood of those devout ones and their death as*
> ***an atoning sacrifice**, divine Providence preserved Israel that*
> *previously had been mistreated* (17:20–22).

Isaiah talks about the suffering servant, Judah, who experiences a kind of death, though that death is metaphorical. The servant is *cut off from the land of the living* (Isa. 53:8), which (obviously) does not describe the literal death of Judah in exile, but the very fact of exile itself—they now live outside of the land, which is the place of death.

But now in 4 Maccabees, the physical death of individual martyrs is the focus. The nation as a whole is ransomed and its sins atoned for by the *death* of the martyrs.

As in the Old Testament, "to ransom" means to "buy back," as when a price is paid to have someone released from captivity, and "to atone" means to supply satisfaction for an offense or injury, as when you make up for or make amends for your sins. How exactly to tie these metaphors to Jesus's crucifixion continues to be a tough nut to crack for Christian theology, but that's not our focus. We just need to see that Jesus individually is described in similar ways as the martyrs are in 4 Maccabees. He gives his life as a *ransom for many* (Matt. 20:28; also 1 Tim. 2:6; 1 Pet. 1:18; Rev. 5:9) and to be an *atoning sacrifice for our sins* (1 John 2:2; 4:10; also Rom. 3:25; Heb. 2:17).

There is no way that that New Testament writers were flipping through 4 Maccabees and thought, "Wow, what a novel idea. This will fit perfectly." Rather, 4 Maccabees shows us that the idea that sin can be atoned for by the suffering of *others* was already "in the air" by the time we get to Jesus. What Christian theologians call "vicarious" or "substitutionary" atonement (Jesus died *instead* of you and *for* you) isn't a new idea in the New Testament.

The new element, though, is that suffering and dying for others is all focused on *one* martyr's death, Jesus's.

Like resurrection, seeing Jesus's death as a sacrifice for others is tied to Old Testament imagery (Isaiah 52–53), but at the same time works off a later act of reimagining what this God of old is about.

In Jesus, martyrdom and messiahship merge. The death of the king redeems and atones for the sins of the world—a radical act of reimagining what God would do.

If we miss the surprise of all this, we miss the drama of the gospel.

A new thing is happening, something that goes beyond the familiar language of old. God is being reimagined. New wineskins are needed.

* * *

The gospel doesn't match up with Israel's story, as if it were an index at the end that lined up with what came before. The gospel is an act of reimagining God in view of an unexpected and ground-shifting development—not exile to Babylon, as formative as that was for Judaism, but a Messiah who challenged central elements of Israel's identity (Law, Temple, land), but who also died a shameful, dishonorable, criminal's death and then was raised.

The New Testament story is, in other words, one big act of wisdom— a response to God's surprising presence here and now.

If we think of the gospel as simply rolling right off the Old Testament tongue, we will be wrong. And we will fail to appreciate how creative the New Testament writers were in working out the day-to-day real-time implications of all of this.

Which brings us back to Paul, the most polarizing figure of the New Testament.

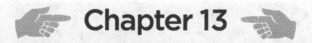

Chapter 13

Figuring
It Out

Reading Someone Else's Mail

We got a new mail carrier a while back. Nice guy. Apparently has trouble reading, though.

I keep getting letters that are clearly intended for someone else, judging by the names and addresses *clearly* marked on the *front* of every piece of mail. This is a problem, big enough, perhaps, for even the US Postal Service to take notice. "Yeah, hi. Listen, I have a letter and small package here for Martha J. Thomson of 418 S. Richardson Avenue, which does not remotely resemble my name or address. Please advise."

That's what I would *like* to say if ever I actually got a live person on the phone at the local branch of the USPS. But instead, I either have to lurk in the bushes and pounce or, if pressed for time, simply stuff it all back in the mailbox and hope the new guy figures it out the next day or two. Still, in an act of petty vengeance, I dug up my curbside mailbox and affixed a new one fifty feet farther away at my front door. That'll learn 'em.

And I hope that whoever might be getting my mail—probably a grubby thirty-five-year-old gamer who never helps around the house and lives off his poor wife's waitressing check—will pay it forward and be diligent and upstanding in returning my mail to me unopened.

Reading someone else's mail is a bit tempting, I have to admit, but if you stop to think about it, apart from being illegal (it is a crime carrying a three-year jail sentence), it is a complete waste of time. And even if the letter lets you in on some sordid personal details, it doesn't matter. What good does it do to know that, say, someone's marriage is falling apart or that kids threw up at Six Flags?

Letters have a context that the sender shares with the addressee. You are neither. The information does you no good. Cut it out.

With that in mind, it has struck me over the years that some of the most important pieces of literature in the entire Bible are

> personal letters
>
> written two thousand years ago
>
> by people I've never met named Paul, Peter, James, John, and some others
>
> and intended for people I absolutely know nothing about
>
> in places I am not remotely familiar with
>
> in a culture I really cannot hope to grasp.

As one of my seminary professors said, "Reading the New Testament is like reading someone else's mail." That might be the most valuable thing I ever learned in seminary. And now I pass it on to you, at a far lower cost.

And yet, this is not mail we are supposed to stuff back in a mailbox. We are *supposed* to read these letters—and not only read them, but find some way to draw them into our own lives.

Think about that for a minute. I think about it a lot.

And it doesn't really matter that we might think these letters are inspired by God. That still leaves the question of why God would decide to inspire context-dependent personal correspondence and expect us to "get it" two thousand years later in a very—I will say it again, *very*—different time and place.

Doesn't God realize that we don't share the common understanding that, say, Paul shares with the people in Corinth or Thessalonica? Doesn't God realize that making twenty-one of the twenty-seven books of the New Testament letters means that we will have to think—really think—about what these letters were meant to do and then be really thoughtful and intentional, maybe even humble, about how to engage them for ourselves?

Doesn't God know that we will have to exercise tremendous— what's that word again? Oh, yes—wisdom in order to know how *or even if* these words will apply to others in their own context-dependent situations?

Leaving the snark aside, I think that letters are the perfect format for a sacred book that is not intended as a helicopter-parenting manual, but as a source of wisdom. We can't simply just drag these letters into our own life as is. We have to work at finding the connection between then and now.

I don't think the value of these letters lies in our ability to ignore their time and place and make believe they were written with us in mind every bit as much as the ancient Jews or Roman citizens they were written to. We get something out of them only by wrestling with their "historical particularity" (as some put it) and then doing the hard work of accepting the sacred responsibility of discerning how all of that works out here and now in whatever situation we find ourselves.

The letters of the New Testament are, to revisit the theme of this book, wisdom documents. We are watching some of the earliest followers of Jesus working out what it meant to walk with God in their moment in time. When we read these letters we are watching wisdom in action.

These letters are not one-size-fits-all documents detached from their ancient moments, ready to touch down just anywhere and anytime without a moment's reflection. We read these letters wisely not when we simply graft the words before us onto an entirely different time and place, but when we study them to see what they are about, for there and then we can see more clearly, guided by wisdom, how we are to bring that biblical wisdom into our here and now.

Of course, this brings us to the apostle Paul, who wrote perhaps as many as thirteen of the twenty-one letters* and who is always easy to understand and never ever says anything controversial. See, I left the snark aside for almost a whole page.

Does God Influence Elections? Dear Lord, I Hope Not

Protestants *love* Paul, because Paul said that we are justified by God's grace and not by works. In Martin Luther's hands, Paul's words launched the Protestant Reformation back in the sixteenth century.

---

* I say "perhaps" because some of Paul's letters, according to most scholars, were likely written later by someone else. That's a complicated issue we don't need to get into here, but I wanted to mention it lest some overzealous doctoral student reading this thinks I am a moron who isn't aware of all this, because, apparently anytime I say anything I have to say everything.

Ever since, Protestants have had an obsessive relationship with the apostle, judging by the fact that, as a lifelong Protestant, I have heard a lot more sermons on Paul than the Gospels (or Old Testament).

Paul is "our guy," and we Protestants continue to expect from him clear direction about what to believe and what to do. And Paul certainly seems to oblige. He has that alluring black-and-white, decisive, uncompromising "just do what I say" quality that some of us just can't get enough of. It's almost as if Paul's letters have become the Protestant version of the Law.

But that's fine, as long as we remember that biblical laws are, as we saw, evasive and fidgety little buggers that don't really tell you what to do. Reading Paul's letters for clear divine guidance is ironic, and has frustrated more than one Bible reader. No wonder Protestants have a long history of splinter groups hating each other over disagreements about what Paul means.

As with the Law, wisdom is needed when reading Paul's letters— perhaps more than with any other biblical writer because so much is expected of him.

We could throw a dart at Paul's letters to see the point. Oh, look! Mine landed on Romans 13:1, which makes the rounds during every presidential election (as long as your candidate wins): *Let every person be subject to the governing authorities; for there is no authority except from God, and those authorities that exist have been instituted by God.*

This raises some questions, like: "Are you serious?"

Not to escalate this too quickly, but does this include Hitler or other genocidal rulers? Do we just goose-step through life and give our "governing authorities" a free pass because their authority is "instituted by God"? How about some wiggle room? And does this include King George III, because if so, the entire United States of America has been operating outside of God's will for two and a half centuries. Were we wrong? (I'm asking for a friend.)

And as I write this, Romans 13:1 recently made the rounds on the American political scene to shield the administration from criticism for separating illegal immigrants from their children at the border—which is just one of many reasons why politicians should not be allowed near a Bible without adult supervision.

But what if politicians are just plain corrupt—accepting bribes, covering up crimes, ordering tax breaks for the rich and tax hikes for the poor, sponsoring racism, and on and on? Is anything God's will just because rulers say so?

Yes, this verse is in the Bible, and yes, Paul doesn't leave room for debate. But Paul's "command" still needs to come under the scrutiny of wisdom—as with everything else we read—so we can discern *how* or *if* it applies to us today in our moment in time.

Yes, even Paul's letters bend the knee to wisdom.

Again, it would help to remember that reading Paul's letters today is quite literally reading someone else's two-thousand-year-old mail; we do *not* share with Paul and his readers their moment in time. Whatever we might think of Paul, he wasn't an idiot; I'm sure he had very good reasons for saying what he says *for his situation*. But it strikes me as very bad form to take Paul's comment written in the context of the early years of the Jesus movement in the Roman Empire (of all places), simply parachute it into the landscape of American politics, and conclude that God never wants us to criticize a sitting president because God put him or her in office.

We can't know exactly what motivated Paul's black-and-white comment, but a factor that shouldn't be ignored is the uneasy recent history of Jews in Rome. Emperor Claudius had exiled Jews from Rome around the year 50 CE and they only recently returned after the emperor's death.

Paul wrote Romans in that setting, and Romans 13:1 may have been a word of wisdom for the church to keep a low profile and not stir up trouble. As the capital of the Roman Empire and therefore the world, Rome was a strategic center for the successful spread of the gospel. The gospel wasn't about overthrowing Rome, and so they needed to play it smart.

Of course, other explanations are possible. Perhaps Paul was playing on the pro-Roman political devotion of at least some of his readers, seeing that one of Paul's main reasons for writing Romans was to raise money (read a little between the lines of Rom. 15:22–33). Whatever the reason—perhaps all the more so because we don't know what it is—it is simplistic to read this verse as universally binding upon all believers at all times and places, regardless of circumstances.

A command for *that* time does not make it a command for *all* time. That can be a hard lesson to accept, especially of Paul, but it is true.

It's possible that Paul is echoing a line of thinking from his Jewish tradition—at least part of it—since the Babylonians were seen by some Old Testament writers as God's instrument for punishment (Jer. 28:14; 29:1–14; Hab. 1:5–11) and the Persian king Cyrus as God's servant for bringing the exiled Jews back home (see Isa. 45:1, 13). Yet Jewish tradition also has a strand that looks forward to the time when the *yoke* of their oppressors will be broken (Isa. 9:4; 10:27; Jer. 30:8). And Jews, let's not forget, rightly rebelled against the wicked king Antiochus IV Epiphanes, which led to a period of (uneasy) Jewish political semi-independence for about a century.

The Jewish tradition includes diverse, context-dependent views on what to think of foreign rule. And with that in mind, it's worth mentioning that Paul was hardly a model of consistency. He also engaged in politically subversive activity, namely, when he declared again and again that Jesus is "Lord." That word carried political as well as religious freight in the Roman Empire; it was a title used for the "divine" Caesar. To speak of another as "Lord," not simply over some people (Jews), but over all people, including Caesar and his subjects, was insurrection, which eventually led to some jail time for Paul; he likely spent his last years under house arrest, ironically in Rome (Acts 28:30–31).

So, for Paul, sometimes you hold your ground and invite Rome's wrath and sometimes you don't—not unlike the choice we saw in Proverbs 26:4–5: sometimes you answer a fool and sometimes you don't.

Far from being an unalterable law that simply has to be obeyed by all at all times because Paul said it and it's in the Bible, Romans 13:1 *is a demonstration of wisdom at work*, of choosing the best path for Paul's here and now. Rather than simply doing what Paul told the Christians in the Roman capital to do two thousand years ago, we today follow Paul best by exercising the same kind of wisdom he did—discerning for ourselves how best to follow God in our time and place.

Slaves, Women, and Homosexuals: No Big Deal, Nothing to See Here

Accepting the invitation of wisdom as we read Paul for today is a responsibility we can never shed. Which brings me to three controversial issues in Paul's letters that have generated enough heat among Christians to melt the moons of Neptune: slaves, women, and homosexuals.*

(Deep breath.)

As for slavery, Paul could have been clearer. He never actually argues for it, but he does assume its legitimacy, as does the Old Testament; he never once calls the institution itself into question and certainly never abolishes it. That being said, major props to Paul for pushing the social boundaries of his day, for example, when he claims that slaves are "equal" to free persons in God's eyes (Gal. 3:28)—which did not accord with the thinking of the ancient Israelites (recall from chapter 3 that slaves did not have the rights of free Israelites).

In a society based on honor and shame, where the social pecking order was sacred, claiming that slaves and free persons were the same in God's eyes would be like telling white supremacists that they are no better in God's eyes than people of color. So Paul is pushing the boundaries. But the church has had a far from flawless track record when it comes to slavery. There are instances that are horrid and shameful throughout the history of Christianity, not least of which is the saga of buying and selling Africans (to the glory of God, of course). And yes, as hard as it is to believe, even today I have heard Christians making atrocious arguments from their rulebook Bible for why slavery of non-white humans is part of God's design.

Having said that, if you asked your average Joe and Jane on the street what Christians think about slavery, they'd probably say that

---

* Technically, Paul says nothing about "homosexuals"; rather, he talks about those who engage in same-sex intercourse. The latter is an act, whereas the former is a modern category that speaks to an "orientation," what someone *is*, which the Bible doesn't cover. I'm using "homosexual" here out of convenience.

Christians denounce slavery as immoral. Generally speaking, in other words, *the church is known for having accepted Paul's boundary-pushing trajectory and pushing it farther.* Freedom and equality eventually won out as the norm over passages like, *Slaves, obey your earthly masters with fear and trembling* (Eph. 6:5), a compliant go-to passage of nineteenth-century Southern slave owners.

Actually, slavery is a really good example for us to look at here. That issue caused a real crisis for Christians in the nineteenth century who thought the Bible held the clear answer. The problem is that Northern abolitionists and Southern anti-abolitionists both made their case by pointing to the same Bible.

The thing is, when the Bible is viewed as a once-for-all rulebook, the anti-abolitionists had a slam-dunk case, because you have passages from both parts of the Bible that assume the institution of slavery. The abolitionists had to argue differently—on the basis of the Bible's trajectory toward justice and equality. That type of argument is a wisdom argument, tied not to the words on the page, but to discerning where the Spirit seems to be leading. I'm glad to say that the wisdom way of handling slavery won the day—at least in theory. The racism that lay beneath is, tragically, still with us.

But my point is that the just way of addressing human slavery had to go *beyond the Bible*—it had to take seriously "the moment" and read it well.

The Bible couldn't be counted on to settle a pressing moral issue of the day—whether God favors light-skinned over dark-skinned humans (if they even *are* human). That should have been a wake-up call to everyone that knowing what to do can't be left to finding a Bible verse.

The Bible isn't set up for that sort of thing. The Bible is ambiguous enough for us to find there what we already believe. The answer to this issue would need to be found elsewhere—in the realm of wisdom, not Bible verses.

The same principle of wisdom holds for Paul's views (plural) on women. Many Christians today and throughout history have clung fast to the view that pastoring, preaching, teaching, and other such ordained authoritative churchly functions are restricted to men, because Paul says things like, *Women should be silent in the churches* (1 Cor. 14:34) and *I permit no woman to teach or to have authority over a man* (1 Tim. 2:12).*

But, not unlike his views on government, Paul seems to be comfortable with multiple options. In Romans 16:1 he entrusts Phoebe to bring his letter to the Roman church and in 16:7 praises a woman named Junia as a prominent apostle, a role often assumed in some Christian circles to be reserved for males. In 1 Corinthians 11:4–5, Paul takes for granted that women *are* praying and prophesying (speaking for God) in public right alongside men rather than being "silent."

The simple fact that Paul isn't consistent about women should *never* be seen as some logical embarrassment to be overcome—like a misprint in a legally binding contract or an owner's manual that has to be corrected—but as a clear sign that *wisdom thinking is at work*. We follow Paul's lead best when we likewise exercise wisdom in our here and now. Christians have always had to choose which

---

* Both passages are thought by most scholars to have been written by someone other than Paul. That doesn't make a huge difference for us here, though some argue that these and some other problem passages can be dismissed for that reason. I think they need to be addressed regardless, if for no other reason than the unwise manner in which these passages have been used.

of Paul's two trajectories to follow, and Christian history is replete with both.

Knowing something of the world Paul lived in may help us see what it means to follow Paul with wisdom rather than as a dispenser of information.

In a rather striking move, we read that husbands and wives should submit to each other: *Be subject to one another out of reverence for Christ* (Eph. 5:21). The words that follow, however, aren't exactly the stuff of women's liberation: *Wives, be subject to your husbands as you are to the Lord* (5:22).* On the social ladder at the time, women had a clearly defined rung—below men. I seriously doubt that "women's rights" as we think of them today were on Paul's radar, given his time and place. Simply lighting a match to the social ladder, as some of us might have hoped he would do, would have gotten him nowhere. A move like that would have actually erected barriers for the Christian mission in that Roman world. Like our trying to start up a community organization that barred women from positions of rank and authority, it would never have gotten off the ground.

Which brings us to an ironic twist that gets right to the heart of reading Paul's letters with wisdom at our side.

Paul's comments about women straddled the line between social expectations of the day and Christian liberation from those expectations. To have obliterated those expectations would have impeded his mission to spread the gospel. Today, cultural expectations are not what they were in the Roman Empire of Paul's time, and it is our responsibility to, likewise, be aware of those expectations

---

* I might as well also mention that Ephesians is another one of those letters that Paul himself may not have written.

and not obliterate them, lest the mission of spreading the gospel be compromised.

And so, taking seriously today Paul's words about women would mean employing the same principle of wisdom, *but arriving at the completely opposite conclusion* about the role and status of women, given our cultural expectations. Paul brought gender equality into his world as far as he could. Christians today can—and should—build on that wise trajectory and take it farther.

A paradox: only by "disobeying" Paul's "command" are we able to follow the path of wisdom he was following.

Finally, whether Christians today should accept same-sex relationships and marriage equality is a lightning rod of controversy (in case you haven't noticed). This issue is, I feel, a complex one in which we need to keep a lot of plates spinning. This isn't the book for working through all that.* Here I just want to point out a self-evident fact: although you will always have your quotient of belligerent people in any Christian debate, most of those involved in this one are good and decent people who disagree about both what the Bible says and what sort of guidance we can expect from the Bible on this issue. At least that is my experience.

As I see it, as in the slavery issue, the side of the sexuality debate that can more easily draw on the Bible for support is the "homosexuality is a sin" side—it's relatively easy to find passages that are negative, but not a single passage that affirms what we call same-sex relation-

---

* Some thoughtful treatments include Matthew Vines, *God and the Gay Christian: The Biblical Case in Support of Same-Sex Relationships* (New York: Convergent, 2014); James V. Brownson, *Bible, Gender, Sexuality: Reframing the Church's Debate on Same-Sex Relationships* (Grand Rapids, MI: Eerdmans, 2009); Dale B. Martin, *Sex and the Single Savior: Gender and Sexuality in Biblical Interpretation* (Louisville: Westminster John Knox, 2006).

ships. But the very fact that polar opposite opinions exist among actual Christians shows us that there is more going on here than what first meets the eye.

In my opinion, digging into Paul's words introduces us to some context-dependent complexities that might not be apparent at first blush. It's not enough to cite, for example, Romans 1:24–27 as clear proof that God hates queers without struggling with how human sexuality was understood in Paul's day.

Paul certainly decries *degrading passions* and "unnatural" acts, and I certainly don't think he would be advocating for Gay Pride Day.

But some argue that the idea of "sexual orientation" was not on anyone's radar back then and so same-sex intercourse was seen not as doing what comes naturally for those born that way, but evidence of being so depraved and sexually out of control that "natural" outlets aren't enough and you spill over to what is "unnatural." Also, one of the men in same-sex intercourse would have to assume the submissive female role (as would one woman the dominant male role), thus exchanging the natural for the unnatural (see Romans 1:26–27).

As with any other issue, we have to consider that Paul's words might not be an eternally binding command, but a comment that assumes a culture of sexuality different from our own.

Further, some see Paul's entire introduction in Romans 1:18–32 as a setup for the rest of the argument in the chapters that follow. Paul seems to be dealing with tensions between Jewish and Gentile followers of Jesus, and a core purpose of the letter is to convince them that they are all on the same page—neither group has higher status than the other. Jews do not get a free pass simply because they are children of Abraham and have Torah. Greeks are not superior simply because they aren't subject to laws like circumcision and eating only clean foods.

In Romans 1, Paul is outlining specifically Greco-Roman types of behaviors beginning with idolatry and sexual depravity and continuing in the Greco-Roman "vice list" in verses 29–31. As a Jew, Paul begins his letter of reconciliation between Jews and Gentiles by slamming Greek culture for being ungodly. And one can perhaps see Paul's fellow Jews listening to this portion of the letter and feeling a bit good about themselves—here is Paul, one of "us," putting these Gentiles in their place. Go get 'em, Paul.

But then Paul turns the tables on his fellow Jews in chapter 2, which he more or less keeps up for the remainder of the letter. Jews, Paul argues, are in no different a place in God's eyes than these depraved Gentiles. Why? Because though they have Torah, they don't actually keep it—which makes them worse off. The punch line (the first of many, actually) comes in Romans 3:22–23: *There is no distinction [between Jew and Gentile], since all have sinned and fall short of the glory of God.*

When Paul says *all have sinned*, we might think he is speaking on the individual level, but he is certainly speaking on the corporate level: instead of *all*, read "both"—meaning both Jews and Gentiles—and then we'll see better what Paul is getting at.

In other words, Paul's opening about "unnatural" acts isn't about laying down some unconnected point about the worst sin ever: "Before I begin, let me just say that God absolutely hates queers." Rather, Paul's comment is a setup. It creates the rhetorical energy Paul needs to unsettle his fellow Jews: even though they do not condone that behavior, they are in fact no better.

My point is that even though Paul's words can't be made to mean anything we like, once we dig in to the cultural context a bit, we see that Paul might mean something other than what we expected.

Whatever else we do, and especially with issues that generate so much conflict, wisdom must be pursued by all and invited to take a prominent place in these discussions—if only so that they may remain discussions and not an exercise in lobbing back and forth "clear" Bible verses as grenades. Using Bible verses to end discussions on difficult and complex issues serves no one and fundamentally misses the dimension of wisdom that is at work *anytime* we open the Bible *anywhere* and read it.

And certainly power plays and intimidation have no place. Rather here, precisely *because* human sexuality is such a divisive issue among Christians, we must be tuned in to the need to seek wisdom together at all costs and with all patience and humility. There is room for pointed debate—but not for verse wars and hatred. Abandoning wisdom is never an option.

Never has been. Never will be.

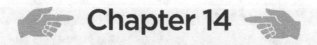

Chapter 14

Grace
and Peace
to You

The God of the Here and Now

So what's my point? You've probably been wondering since page 3.

What we've seen in chapters 1–13 is a normal part of Christianity, past and present. Christians, just like their Jewish ancestors, have always been reimagining God, adapting the sacred past to discern God's presence here and now. And we can never simply appeal to the Bible as an unchanging standard, for the Bible itself—Old and New Testaments alike—never sits still. Its authors have already accepted their sacred responsibility to employ wisdom.

As should we—always respectful of the past, but never assuming that we are meant to recreate it and live in it; always tied to this ancient tradition, but without expecting it to do the heavy lifting for us.

The life of faith has always been about respecting this tension and living by wisdom.

Earlier in the book I confessed that I no longer think of God as "up there," because my experience won't let me. For me, there is no "up" above a flat earth in a small cosmos topped with a dome. This is where ancient Israelites might have imagined God to be, and they communed with God by those images authentically. But let's not forget that those very images were part of their ancient Mesopotamian world. Other than to put myself in their place as an intellectual exercise, I cannot believe as they did. I live in a different world.

My view of God has to take into account the reality I live in in order to be authentic here and now. I think of God not as taking up space somewhere far away, but as ever-present Spirit—not one to be discovered "out there" who makes occasional appearances in burning bushes, dreams, or a select few prophets, but as one always present and to whom I need to be awakened daily. Of course, that's just me, though I am hardly alone in conceiving of God this way. In fact, this understanding of God is already part of the biblical trajectory,* though it also leaves some of it aside.

No part of my faith can steer clear from wisdom questions: "What is God like here and now?" "What do I mean when I say 'God?'" "What does it mean to believe and trust in this God?" And all those questions have their own flavor depending on who is asking them, when, and where.

I ponder these questions by taking seriously this ancient, ambiguous, and diverse Bible we have as well as honoring my humanity—my experiences, my reasoning, when and where I was born—and I try to get all these factors to talk to each other. That may ring a bell with some of you. I am echoing the so-called Wesleyan Quadrilateral. We are always processing God and faith not from a high place, but from the vantage point of our inescapable humanity—our reason, experience, tradition, and scripture. (The Episcopal Three-Legged Stool is similar, but it combines reason and experience.)

---

* *But will God indeed dwell on the earth? Even heaven and the highest heaven cannot contain you, much less this house that I have built!* (1 Kings 8:27); *Am I a God near by, says the LORD, and not a God far off? Who can hide in secret places so that I cannot see them? says the LORD. Do I not fill heaven and earth? says the LORD* (Jer. 23:23–24).

And in the midst of all that sometimes exhilarating, sometimes anxiety-provoking, but never dull work of wisdom, I have come to believe that this God we speak of, if this God is worthy of the name *love*, is not surprised or put off by our human limitations, even if some around us are. This God is not shocked when we "don't get it," but understands who we are and what we are and is fine with it.

If the incarnation is true—God with us in Jesus of Nazareth—what else could we say? If this core mystery of the Christian faith (which I believe can never be truly articulated) is true, and that the Creator not only took part in the human drama, but suffered in that drama, perhaps we have an understanding and compassionate God, not one out to get us?

Maybe it's all good.

That's really my point. As I said near the beginning, this book may be called *How the Bible* Actually *Works*, but the deeper topic is how we think about God here and now. Processing that question happens in the arena of wisdom, which, as the Bible shows us, has always been the case—whether we are talking about fools, wealth, or slave laws; whether children are punished or rewarded for their parents' deeds; whether Manasseh or the Assyrians repented; whether the exile will ever end. All these questions are really about what God is like.

That was the struggle of the ancient Israelites, like the psalmists who pleaded with God to deliver them from their enemies.

That was the struggle of the Judahites in exile as they pondered what kind of God would do this and whether it will ever be over.

That was the struggle of Jews living under the thumb of the Greek and Roman Empires, seeking how to be faithful to the past while living in a world that the past never accounted for.

And that is the struggle of the New Testament writers, as they sought to understand how the new wine of the gospel and the old wineskin of Israel's ancient tradition can coexist.

The Christian tradition has always been about the business of re-imagining God, of following this trajectory laid out for us in scripture.

Drop a pin anywhere on the timeline of Christian history, even the earliest stages, and we will see without fail people of faith adapting the tradition to speak to their here and now.

Christians began writing creeds perhaps as early as the second century, though that practice owed little to the Jewish heritage that bore the Jesus movement and more to Greek and Latin philosophy. And that's fine. That's the form the Christian faith took in that time and place. That was the world of ancient credal Christians, and they put the gospel into words in ways that reflected that world.

As if there were another option.

But these creeds are not high moments of the Christian tradition simply to be recited as if that's the end of it, though they tend to be seen as that. Rather, they are monuments to wisdom that we revisit with profit, but dare not hold up as the nonnegotiable high moment of the tradition. That place is taken by Jesus, the true subject that all creeds are trying to put into words.

The same goes for any other stage of this Christian tradition—including the one any of us might happen to hold dear. The medieval church had a long history of struggling with how to read the Bible for spiritual value and gave us four "methods" for doing so: the Bible can be understood literally, allegorically, morally, or prophetically. So the exodus, for example, isn't just literally about release from Egyptian bondage. Allegorically it points us to redemption in Christ. Morally it symbolizes personal conversion from sin to grace. Prophetically it points to our leaving the bondage of this world and moving on to the next.

This "Fourfold Method," as it's called, didn't just pop up out of nowhere, but grew over centuries as pilgrims asked how this Bible can help along this journey. I don't feel I can or should ignore their wisdom, but neither can I long for a time gone by as if it held the secret key. I have my own context to deal with, as they did theirs. I have my own sacred responsibility.

The broad movement known as the Protestant Reformation wasn't dropped out of heaven to correct fifteen hundred years of bad Catholic theology (which is what some Protestants think). It was a movement for its time that grew out of all sorts of political, geographical, and ecclesiastical complexities. Good certainly came from it, but to think that sixteenth-century Europe is where God has spoken most clearly and that the church's task today is to form coalitions to recover the "spirit of the Reformation" is, ironically, not in keeping with the wisdom that the Bible models for us.

Wisdom leads us to dialogues with the past. It doesn't lead us back to the past.

The Challenge of Wisdom

Christians today, living when and where we are, have no choice but to be intentional in following the Bible and the entire history of Christianity in accepting the sacred responsibility to ask how we can talk about God in a way that is both connected to the tradition and meaningful for today. It is most fair to ask whether at some point we will cross the line from adapting the tradition to obscuring it. But the fact that this concern is valid does not mean we can avoid the wisdom task altogether. The life of faith isn't that easy.

But I am reminded again of the Bible itself and how its portraits of God are deeply rooted in the cultures of the time. When Yahweh is described as a mighty warrior who slays the enemy, or a sovereign king who makes treaties with his people, or male, or seated in the midst of a divine council of gods, I am reminded that there is no God-talk that can keep its distance from our humanity. All our language of God, including that of the biblical writers, is inescapably enmeshed with how people of any time think and talk about anything—even as they speak of One who is not bound by time and place.

Even the climax of the story for Christians—Jesus—is expressed in the language of the time as it tells a story that transcends time. Jesus is called Lord, Savior, and bringer of the Good News of peace and grace—all of which mimics the language of the Roman Empire to speak of glorious Caesar as a means of pointing beyond Caesar. The Greek word for god, *theos*, was used to speak of Zeus and the other gods; the New Testament writers use it to speak of their God alone as the true God. Jesus was Messiah, a Jewish royal term charged with political meaning, but redefined around suffering, death, resurrection, and hope for all humanity.

Whatever any of us think about the Bible as God's inspired word, it should make us take a step back and reflect for a moment that scripture itself portrays the boundless God in culturally bound ways of thinking.

And all that brings me to ask the question that I have been asking over and over again, it seems, throughout this book in one way or another: *If that is how the Bible itself actually behaves, who are we to think that the Bible's purpose is to have us step around our own sacred responsibility to reimagine God rather than warmly embrace it?*

If that notion is still a bit unnerving for some, as I can well understand, look on the bright side. We are all already doing that very thing whenever we talk about God—and the biblical writers were already doing that very same thing long before any of us came on the scene.

Whatever fear there might be, grace and peace are also to be found by taking the Bible seriously enough to accept the challenge of wisdom and truly own our faith here and now. That, as I've been saying, is our sacred responsibility, and by accepting that responsibility we will learn to let go of the youthful fear of the unfamiliar and move toward wisdom and maturity.

That, I believe, is what God wants for us. After all, God is not a helicopter parent.

Acknowledgments

I'm not an island, though I do hope to own one someday.

I write in community, primarily as a member of a family. No, my wife, Sue, and our three grown offspring, Erich, Lizz, and Sophie, don't actually do any of my writing. They're busy people—though I should say that Sue read the page proofs and caught dozens of errors and said, "I think this is your best book." So there you go. Anyway, my family is always *there*, and every word I write is as a member of this now growing family and feeds off of this immeasurable blessing, which has been the center of my life, now pushing thirty-five years, and means more to me than writing books.

My sincere debt of thanks goes to my agent, Kathryn Helmers, at Creative Trust, who—as she may recall—I had to pester for a year before she agreed to take me on. And I'm glad she did. Kathy gets what I'm trying to say before I know it myself. And speaking of which, the team at HarperOne is amazing (and fun) to work with. Mickey Maudlin, my editor, has such a knack for seeing what I'm getting at that I've begun to wonder whether this was in fact the reason why he was put on this earth. He also has unparalleled skill for finding kind ways of saying, "I have no idea what you're trying to say here" (me neither) or "Do you even *have* a book concept?" (you tell me). Assistant editor Anna Paustenbach lent many insightful observations, and *always* kept things running smoothly in this unwieldy process of writing and editing. Production editor Lisa Zuniga gracefully made sure we stayed on schedule toward the end. Courtney

Acknowledgments

Nobile in publicity and Jenn Jensen and Kalie Caetano in marketing are to be commended for putting their careers and reputations on the line by working with me.

Oh, and the team is even bigger. Thanks to the guys who waterproofed my basement and replaced my sewer line so I wouldn't have to. Thanks to my student Will Abbott for helping me shingle a roof, and my colleague Eric Flett for helping me replumb my entire house and paint my basement floor. You all helped me salvage some time to finish the book almost on time. *Highlights* magazine—yes, the children's magazine—has this great conference center where I spent a week in a cabin (how writer-ish of me) in the hope of getting some clarity on where in heaven's name this book was going. And it worked. And the great food and (free) wine and beer didn't hurt either. My former students Michelle Miles and Alyssa Welty graciously agreed to read the final proofs in a timely manner and (though noting "you're really being sarcastic here") didn't utter a single negative word even though this could have been major payback time. And finally, Shay Bocks somehow managed to create a beautiful timeline and maps based on my unreasonable, even incomprehensible, instructions ("No, no, I want it to look like, really good, with like curvy arrows and banners or something, but not *too* curvy or bannery. And we need it by tomorrow."), even while surrounded by her three young boys.

Whenever I think, write, and teach on the topic of scripture, I am mindful of those through the years who have enlightened and motivated me to think better thoughts. I am often asked who my favorite scholars or books are, and I am never able to give a straight answer. There have been too many, and what constitutes "favorite" tends to change over time. But I would like to mention two of my doctoral

Acknowledgments

professors, James Kugel and Jon Levenson. Without realizing it, they modeled for this sheltered Protestant what it means to read the Bible closely and on its own terms, rather than seeking from it the comfort of arriving at familiar conclusions. Their influence has shaped much of my thinking and I remain in their debt nearly thirty years later. I hope some portion of what they taught me has been passed on to my unsuspecting students over the years.

All of which is to say, this book has been a team effort. I hope those reading it will find some encouragement in its pages.

Finally, to my wonderful granddaughter, Lilah, to whom this book is dedicated. Not only is she a cutie buns, but she tirelessly looked over several versions of this book and spit up on several of them. I couldn't have done this without you—though I might have gotten done a bit sooner.

Scripture Index

Old Testament

Scripture Index

Apocrypha

Scripture Index

New Testament

Subject Index

Abraham and Sarah, 7, 220, 224, 233, 237

Adam and Eve, 39, 40, 42, 187, 219, 245

adaptation: honoring religious tradition through, 165–66, 187–90; New York Yankees' example of successful, 216–17; survival requires, 163–65. *See also* biblical adaptation

Alexander the Great, 108, 173

ambiguous/ambiguity of the Bible: Bible characteristic of, 5–6, 8, 12, 19; of the biblical laws, 52, 53–54, 58–59, 64–65, 67–68; book of Proverbs as being, 35–38, 76; pondering questions about God in context of, 272; of the Ten Commandments, 58–59; wise adaptation of biblical laws in diversity from, 69–71

ancient/antiquity of the Bible: Bible characteristic of, 5–6, 8, 12, 19; book of Proverbs as being, 35–38, 76; pondering questions about God in context of, 272

angels, 183–85

animal-sitting rules, 52–53

Antiochus IV Epiphanes, King, 181–82, 259

Aramaic language, 172–73

Assyria, 85–86, 99, 102–6, 110, 232

atonement, 249

authority of governing authorities, 257–60

Baal (Canaanite god), 168

Babylonian exile: Adam and Eve's, 39, 40; of children due to their parents' sins, 89–92; of Judah to Babylon, 39–40, 105–6, 232–33; NT connecting Jesus's ministry to return from, 242–46; panic and pain of the Israelites', 98–100, 230–31; people of Judah returned from their, 100, 233; reimagining of God following the, 168–69; resurrection as OT metaphor for returning from, 241–42; 2 Chronicles on King Manasseh and the, 109–12, 273; triggering the writing of OT, 101–2, 169–73. *See also*

Jewish people; kingdom of Judah

Babylonian Talmud, 106

baptism of Jesus, 209–10

Bathsheba, 231–32

Ben Sira, 61–62

Bible: as a conversation and debate over time, 77; crisis of God's abandonment triggering writing of, 101–2, 169–73; danger of a rulebook view of the, 27–28, 78; finding better ways to read the, 15–19; how it does and does not help with child rearing, 24–28; how it is used to justify opposite positions, 10; introduction to the *ancient, ambiguous,* and *diverse* nature of the, 5–9, 12; languages of the, 127; on the laws given to Israel by God, 51–52; our misguided expectations of the, 3–5; passages on life and death in the, 39–40; spiritual adaptation as key to understanding wisdom of the, 78–82; various images of God in the, 153–54. *See also*